To Darien
Merry Christmas
from Mom
1990

HOT HATCHBACKS

HOT HATCHBACKS

THE SUCCESSFUL MODEL DESIGN OF THE 1980'S

by
William Kimberley

WILLIAM KIMBERLEY LIMITED
LONDON

ACKNOWLEDGEMENTS

ACKNOWLEDGEMENTS ─────────────────────────────

The author would like to thank the following who greatly contributed to this publication.

Antonella Albanese of Fiat Auto (UK) Ltd.
Juliette Brindley of V.A.G. (UK) Ltd.
Paul Buckett of Citroen Cars Ltd.
Geoffrey Charles of Renault (UK) Ltd.
Helen Davies of Citroen Cars Ltd.
Beverley Gale of V.A.G. (UK) Ltd.
David Mills of The Colt Car Co. Ltd.
N. Barrington Needham, formerly of Alfa Romeo (GB) Ltd.
Barry Reynolds of The Ford Motor Company and
Pam Wearing of Austin Rover Group Limited.

and special thanks to Anne Hope of Motor Industry Archives.

© William Kimberley, 1987

All rights reserved. No part of this book may be reproduced or transmitted in any form or by any means, electronic or mechanical, including photocopying, recording or by any information storage or retrieval system, without permission of William Kimberley Limited.

Printed in England by The Lavenham Press Limited.

CONTENTS

Introduction		6
Chapter One	Early Days	8
Chapter Two	The Competition Hots Up	22
Chapter Three	The Stakes are Raised	42
Chapter Four	The Going gets Tough	74
Chapter Five	Variations on a Theme	96
Chapter Six	The New Wave	140
Specifications		162

INTRODUCTION

It is but 10 short years since the original Golf GTi made its first public appearance, but in that time, it has carved out not only for itself, but for its followers and imitators, a whole new area for their manufacturers to chase sales and gain macho kudos.

The hatchback was a design phenomenon that began to take off in popularity in the mid-seventies. The reason was easy to see. Its opening rear door added an extra dimension to that of most motor cars, and together with the fold-down rear seats, a luggage space was created larger than any saloon could hope to offer.

That such a style of car should become the focus of attention of the enthusiast and sporting driver was something of a surprise, for it was so different from previous sporting machines which tended to be either small open sports cars or exotic expensive supercars, apart from a few exceptions.

Many of the early hot hatchbacks were borne out of a manufacturer's desire to have a car on which to base a rally weapon. This was why the Volkswagen management assented to their enthusiastic engineers' concept of the standard Golf. And still today hot hatchbacks are being manufactured for this reason, with the offering from Mazda, the 323 Turbo 4×4 being one of the latest examples, although technologically light years away from the original Golf GTi (although not necessarily better).

Ford's XR3, however, was slightly different as it was built to top off the new Escort range with a sporting version, a practice they had pursued for very many years. Such was the sales success of this car, though, that it helped widen the demand for performance-orientated hatchbacks.

As you thumb your way through this book, you will notice just how far advanced most cars have become over the 10 years. The state of the art hatchback now has either a turbocharger or a 16-valve unit, and four-wheel drive is now entering the equation.

As an enthusiast the joy of driving almost all these hot hatchbacks at some stage was in itself a major reason for writing the book, and whenever my spell with a car came to an end, my heart sank . . . until the next one came along.

One of the biggest problems was to try and define just what exactly a hot hatchback was. Should the Ford Sierra Cosworth qualify; after all it has a hatchback and is undoubtedly super-quick, and what about a Porsche 944 Turbo. I have mostly relied on what the manufacturers classify as being their sporting hatchbacks and feel that no model has unjustly been left out or included.

William Kimberley
January, 1987

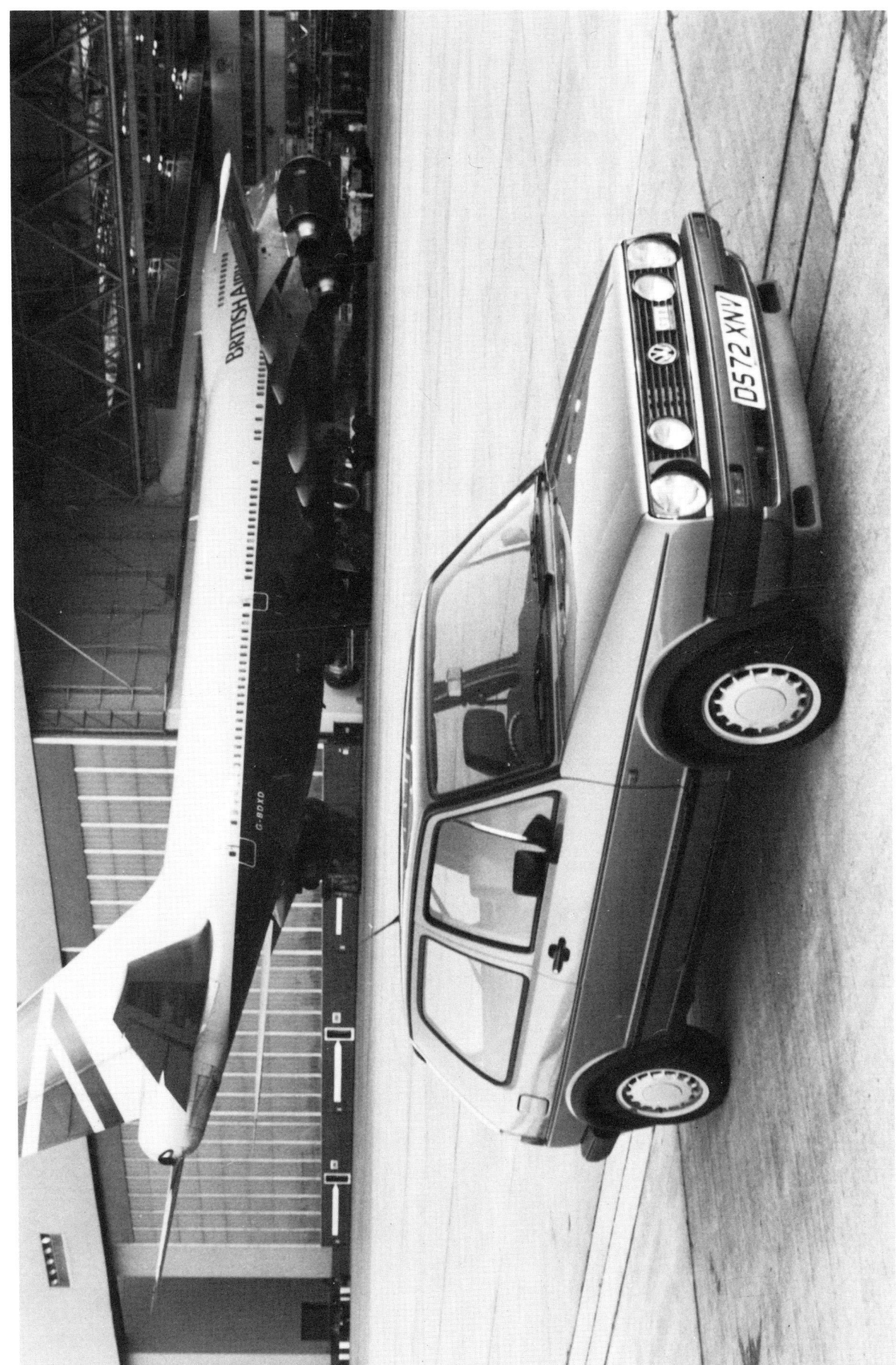

CHAPTER ONE

EARLY DAYS

Hot Hatchbacks are a phenomenon of the 'Eighties, although the design does, in fact, easily pre-date the decade. That Renault had a hatchback design in 1923 has often been overlooked in this decade when it has become the most fashionable style of car. To many of the public, one of the earliest hatchbacks was the Austin A40. One remembers with affection the Farina-designed little car, a relatively unacknowledged landmark design of the 1950s, and it is from this famous design house that some of the original thinking behind the hatchback or "tumble-home", as it was known then, can be traced.

Although not having an opening rear door, the Austin/Morris 1100 with its crisp and pleasing lines, was Pininfarina's continuation of the theme. But by now BMC had decided that the arrangement with the Italian coachbuilders had become outdated and so brought their association to an end.

BMC were years ahead of their rivals when developing the A40 with the aid of Pininfarina in the mid-fifties. With a rear wash/wipe system being too expensive to install, the tail fins were extended to create air turbulence at the rear in an effort to enable the rear screen to self-clean. Although up to six cars were made with a full tail-gate, the car was made with a split hatch. It appeared just before the arrival of the Issigonis Mini and subsequently was ever in its shadow.

The Maxi was BMC's next hatchback, although by no means a hot one. It came about more through a negative edict than a positive one. George Harriman had laid down the rule that BMC were not to have a head-on confrontation with Ford and their Cortina. Since this popular model was a small family saloon, it rather restricted the designers to what they could produce for the gap in their model range between the 1100 and the 1800 which was at present being filled by the worthy, but ageing, Farina-designed Oxford and Cambridge saloons. Another restriction placed in the way of the stylists' flowing pen was the fact that this model was to utilise the 1800's doors.

To get around the edict about the Ford Cortina, BMC's people came up with the tailgate which was about the only appealing feature in a car that was terrible to look at, awful ergonomics, poor performance and horrendous gearbox. To cap it all, the car's launch was delayed so long that in fact it was the first model from British Leyland.

It was from France in 1966, though, that the next great impetus of this style of car came. Although it was a 4-door saloon, the Renault 16 had a lift-up back window similar to that of the Hillman Imp. Its styling, however, was truly different to any of its contemporaries and it can be regarded as the forerunner of today's hatchbacks. At the time its unusual design was even regarded by some as a gimmick allowing Renault to draw attention to their re-entry into the medium-size car market. It was, however, a design that the Regie were taking very seriously, and the car itself really was very good. It was practical, quiet, very economical and, for its time, had an excellent performance.

Its 1470cc engine (76 x 81mm) developed 63bhp at 5,000rpm giving the car a top speed of 90mph and taking 21 seconds to do a quarter of a mile from a standing start. This may not sound electrifying when compared to today's Renault 5TSE, but compared to its contemporaries, it was rapid enough.

The semi air dam that was fitted on the Renault 16 was an idea borrowed directly from the aircraft industry. With the rear window slightly sunken in, a smooth air flow over the rear was maintained.

EARLY DAYS

Inside it was spacious and comfortable but the ergonomics were something to be desired. Its speedometer was calibrated at 5, 20, 35, 50, 65, 80, 95 and 110mph and the pull-up-and-twist handbrake was located on the right hand side. The gear handle was to be found on the left hand side of the steering column.

On the road, the car was commendably quiet and the ride comfortable, but if pressed, it could corner very rapidly indeed. Over rough roads, the suspension was not quite up to the job letting the car grate over the ruts. However, it was a quite outstanding family car, and at £948 17s. 11d. represented good value for money. As an aside, it is worth noting that in 1965, the year before the 16 was introduced, France exported £4,811,000-worth of vehicles to Britain and the UK in return exported £13,017,000-worth of vehicles to France.

Although not quite a hatchback, a performance version of the Hillman Imp was announced at the 1966 Paris Show. Priced at £665 including tax, the Sunbeam Imp Sport had a top speed of 90mph and a 0-60 acceleration of 18 seconds. With twin Stromberg carburettors the 875cc engine developed 51bhp at 6,100rpm.

Utilising this same engine was the Sunbeam Stiletto, a development of the Imp Sport, announced two years later. As it turned out, this design was taking the Rootes Group up a cul-de-sac as it was to prove impossible to develop the rear-engined, rear-wheel drive car into a transversely mounted, front-wheel drive version which turned out to be the definitive style of the hatchback.

The same year the French were at it again. The Simca 1100 was a hatchback for the small car market with an engine developing 2bhp more than the Imp Sport engine giving adequate performance.

It took two years for the 1100 Special and the 1204 development offshoots to be announced. These were sportier versions of their parent, with the Special having one carburettor and the 1204 double Webers enabling them to travel at just under the ton.

The success of the Simca 1100 range in France led to other manufacturers trying their hand with similar cars. Peugeot's hatchback was the 204 model, announced in 1970, with a hot version, the 304 coupe coming out a year later. Its 1300cc engine gave it a top speed the same as the Simca 1100 Special and 1204. A year later, Fiat produced the 127 Sport, a hot hatchback development of the 128.

It was a model from Germany, though, which stole the Brussels Show in 1971, but which since has always been overshadowed by its sister models.

The BMW Touring 2000 tii was an all-new body design. With its saloon car appearance, it looked at a glance like a lower and narrower 2002 tii from the front, but wander round to the rear and you would find its upward-opening rear door. It was the first German car to feature this since the Glas 1004CL/1304CL shown at Frankfurt in 1966. As this marque had been taken over by BMW in that year, it was probable that the design impetus had come from their direction.

The Simca 1100Ti was a car for the budding rally driver and featured a higher ground clearance and rally-type tyres.

The BMW Touring was one of the first sports cars/family saloons/estate cars rolled into one.

The 2 litre engine developed a healthy 130bhp giving it a top speed of 118mph - quite considerably faster than anything vaguely comparable to it. A vacuum-servo disc/drum brake system was employed to be able to stop effectively this, the first, of the truly hot hatchbacks.

It was up the autobahn from Munich that concern was being shown about their own model range. Rudolf Leiding had just taken over as boss of Volkswagen and found that the company was still relying on the ageing Beetle for the bulk of its sales. It was true that it had been updated and cleverly marketed, but the time had come for a replacement. Finding that the work in hand on a future model was not what he thought the company required, he hastily cancelled the project.

At this time, in 1971, engineers from the Audi-NSU side of the concern were working on a model that was to slot in as the base model of the Audi range. It was this which was to be the emergency replacement for the Beetle and the cancelled project. Giorgio Giugiaro of Ital Design was contracted to provide the bodyshell design.

The result that was the Golf took its bow in May 1974 along with the Scirocco, also from the hand of Giugiaro. So strong was the original Pininfarina design for this medium small size of car as seen in their work for BMC that you could still see the influence of Pininfarina thinking.

Straightaway the competition boys saw its potential as a performance car. At that time, the only cars with any sort of sports pretensions were the two seaters, the homologation specials and the exotics.

Its modern single-overhead cam engine with aluminium alloy cylinder head, MacPherson strut suspension and stiff and light bodyshell leant itself perfectly for sporting purposes.

With work being carried out in their own spare time, the engineers showed the results of their labour a few months later in 1974 to Professor Fiala, then head of Research and Development. As far as he and his colleagues were concerned, it was an interesting exercise but 'don't call us, we'll call you.'

Still the enthusiastic engineers played with their baby. They stroked the 1.5 Audi 80 unit to a near-square 79.5 x 80mm giving a capacity of 1588cc. Its Bosch K-Jetronic fuel injection and other modifications now enabled the engine to produce 110bhp, nearly 60 per cent more than the 1.5 litre unit found in the standard Golf. The chassis was fine tuned with brakes and tyres coming in for closer scrutiny.

A year later the engineers called back. This time the fruit of their labour was rewarded. The hierarchy decided to give the green light on a limited run of 5000 examples with a view to homologating the car for Group 1 racing.

EARLY DAYS

The VW Golf GTi's handling was a revelation compared to other small family saloons around at the time.

First public appearance of the car was at the 1975 Frankfurt Show. It was shown more as an engineering exercise and lacked the appendages that make a car go faster, such as the stripes and spoiler.

However, on the car's model launch in June, 1976, it had gained a bib spoiler, alloy wheels and a better interior. The Golf Sport had also now become the GTI.

It was to be another three years before it went on sale in Britain. 1183 four-speed cars were sold before the revised five-speed took its bow in November, 1979. By 1980 over 140,000 examples had been built but only 2,200 of these had been sold in the UK, the problem being that of supplying right-hand drive cars for the market. Its makers were taken aback by the car's instant commercial success.

The success of the Golf GTi opened up a whole new market area for car manufacturers, particularly in sports-orientated Europe. Between the latter half of the 1970's to the end of 1980, car registrations tripled from 70,000 to 200,000.

Although not the first hot hatchback around, it must be acknowledged that the Golf GTI was the car that prodded other large scale manufacturers into going for this important market segment.

The ultimate Q-car, the Golf GTi was the early pacesetter with regard to style, handling, design and desirability and right through to the mid-eighties retained its position as yardstick for its class rivals. For a manufacturer that was stuck with the Beetle for so many years and not having any sort of sporting image, the Golf GTi was a revelation. Yet now that Volkswagen had gone over to front-wheel drive and water-cooled engine, like most conventional manufacturers, its GTi still oozed with the individuality that the Beetle had.

From the word go, it looked a giant-killer. Weighing in at just 1786lb, its 1588cc engine developed 110bhp at 6100rpm, with its torque peaking at 103lb/ft at 5000rpm. Essentially a car for going places fast, for the family man the GTi was both practical and easy to use in town, the engine's outstanding flexibility and marvellous smoothness making it a pleasant car to drive in heavy traffic. It was a very complete and handy package.

It was on the open road, though, that the true character of the car could be appreciated. Along country roads its precision and responsiveness shone through. The handling was dead neutral, giving way to the inside rear wheel lifting followed by a lightning fast tail end breakaway. By this point however, you had to be going far faster than wisdom allowed, but by keeping your foot hard on the power and a quick dab of opposite lock, the tail would come straight back as tidily as every other aspect of the Golf's handling.

The heart of the matter was the engine. Its four cylinder engine was a gem being infinitely smooth, powerful and responsive, longing to be revved and urging you to do so. The introduction of the fifth gear in the box in 1979, soon after its introduction in Britain, was a pure delight, matching its power and torque characteristics. The ratios lead beautifully to the next so that acceleration was hard and uninterrupted helped by the short-travel gear lever and quick action clutch.

The success of the Golf GTi was not going by unnoticed. Ford had always maintained a sporting image through its racing connections and model line up. The XR3 was not only Ford's answer to the GTi, it was an equivalent in their new front-drive Escort to the previous Escort RS2000.

Uwe Bahnsen and his design team took the new 1.6 single overhead cam CVH (Compound Value Angle Hemispherical Chamber) engine from the Escort range as the basis of the new model. The use of a twin-choke Weber, instead of Ford's own VV, and a special camshaft increased the output from 79bhp to 96bhp, and torque from 92 to 98lb/ft. This compared to 110bhp at 5500rpm and 119lb/ft at 4000rpm of the RS2000. Where acceleration for the RS2000 to 60mph was 8.6 secs., the smaller engined XR3 did it in 9.5 secs. Due to its superior aerodynamics, however, its top speed was slightly faster, reaching 113mph against 111mph of the older model.

With the benefit of Pirelli P6s as standard, the XR3 enjoyed tremendous roadholding and even on the limit, when the inside rear wheel was beginning to lift, understeer was negligible. Steering, though, was heavy, especially at parking speeds, but was to be expected with a small diameter steering wheel.

It was the suspension, though, that was to prove a problem. Alongside the Golf, it was very much second best. Handicapped by not having been tested on an 'in-house' testing ground, the car had a dreadfully choppy ride that almost proved its undoing. Although acceptable while cruising around town, once on the open road, it developed a harsh and jarring motion pitching about alarmingly. Although not admitted to at the time, such was Ford's consternation that they immediately began re-development of the suspension. The car was thus introduced a year later, but it was still wrong. Instead of being choppy, the car now tended to wallow around.

This fault, however, did not hold back initial sales when the original model was introduced in September, 1981. The good looking car exceeded Ford's expectations with over 25,000 cars being sold, mainly in 1981 and 1982.

The XR3 was the sporting version of the Ford Escort range and in that role followed the footsteps of the RS2000.

EARLY DAYS

One could not escape the fact, though, that although it possessed the potential to beat the VW both on the road and in the showroom when price, looks, spaciousness, cabin design and cornering power were taken into consideration, it was still outranked by the GTi because of its appalling ride and high noise factor from an objectionable boom when driven near the red line.

It was not until the advent of the Escort RS1600i that Ford had a car that could at least be compared to the Golf, but it was never meant as a mainstream model in a specialised market. Developed as a Group A homologation special, where 5,000 models were required, Ford sold a surprising 2,500 models in Britain in 1983.

As this was, however, a very specialist hot hatchback where sales were never expected to be of a great volume, its appearance was not of any real threat to the Golf GTi, except that it did show what the Ford Motor Company were capable of if they put their collective mind to it.

Opposition to the Golf GTi did not come solely from this American multinational. Although the RS1600i was a homologation special and owed its existence to the XR3, General Motors, in the guise of Vauxhall, had already been down this route.

General Motors introduced the T-car, the Vauxhall Chevette in Britain, at the Geneva Show in March, 1975, which Dealer Team Vauxhall developed into the fire-breathing 2300HS two years later. Following success on the rally circuits with this model, a twin-cam, 16-valve development of the 2.3 litre engine, married to a five-speed ZF gearbox, was offered to the public. It had a limited production run of just two years and was available in any colour as long as it was metallic silver. For this comparative uniqueness, it was over twice the price of the base Chevette, selling for £5,312 compared to £2,341. It was never intended as a rival to the Golf GTi, more as a marketing exercise to add some glamour to the Vauxhall model line-up. General Motors' response to the GTi was to come at a later time.

The Vauxhall Chevette 2300HS was little more than a slightly refined version of the 2300HSR rally car and was produced for homologation purposes.

Renault were another manufacturer who were to offer a high performing version of a standard model to further their sporting connections. When introduced into Britain in 1979, Renault had completed a year and a half of sporting successes. The Renault 5 Turbo had come second and third in the 1978 Monte Carlo rally, an A442B had won the famous Le Mans 24-Hour race in June, their Formula One effort was becoming a force to be reckoned with and they had won Group 2 in the 1979 Monte.

Their first sporty offering, based on the 5, was the Alpine which became available in 1975. It was named the Alpine in France as a tribute to the Dieppe factory which did so much of the engine development work. As Chrysler owned the Alpine name in Britain, the model was christened the Renault 5 Gordini, in honour of Amedee Gordini, the man who did so much to make little Renaults go faster, when it came to the UK in the Spring of 1979.

Its engine was the 1289cc unit from the 5TS and the 12. By increasing the bore 3mm to 76mm and retaining the same 77mm stroke, its capacity was increased to 1397cc. Fed by a twin-choke Weber 32DIR58, it developed 93bhp at 6400rpm with maximum torque of 85.4lb/ft at 4000rpm. This was transmitted via a five-speed gearbox as used in the 16TX and 17TS.

Its performance was impressive for it reached 60mph in 10.7 secs. and had a top speed of 107mph. With the feel and response of a sports car, it was a car that asked to be driven hard, but even despite this it was not thirsty with a 30mpg figure easily obtainable. Its peaky engine, however, demanded plenty of gearchanging in order to get the best from it.

The handling was superb as long as the steering was smooth and the line maintained, but should the line be suddenly altered whilst in mid-corner, then the Gordini could turn into a little monster, pushing its tail right out and tucking its nose into the corner. Where ride could be expected to be taut and stiff, it was well-damped and equivalent to the rest of the 5 range.

The Renault 5 Alpine/Gordini was another car associated with rallying, but it was also a fairly civilised road car.

EARLY DAYS

In order to further back-up the kudos gained from the rally cars, Renault decided to market a road-going version of the mid-engined car. It had little in common with ordinary R5s, but by sharing the same name it was a boon to Renault salesmen. Were it not for marketing reasons, doubtless the final shape would have looked more like an exotic supercar, which to all intents and purposes it was, than the 5, thereby suffering a terrible drag co-efficient of 0.46. Its 1397cc turbocharged engine, cradled in a monocoque shell, developed 160bhp at 6000rpm but like the Vauxhall 2300HS and the Escort RS1600i, was meant no more than to be a homologation special for competition purposes.

The road car was developed by Renault's Bureau d'Etudes et de Recherches Exploratoire (BEREX) under Henri Lherm and test driver Alain Serpaggi and only marginally differed from the competition version. The turbo route was chosen after the 2.6 V6 was rejected because it was too heavy and the Douvrin 2.0 litre was too long. That such horsepower could be extracted from the little 1397cc engine was a credit to the Renault engineers who actually managed to obtain 15bhp more than the 2.0 litre Saab turbo.

Because of the great extension to the wheel arches, the turbo was 10 inches wider than the standard car, and altogether there were something like an additional 13 vents into the bodywork to allow air to circulate.

Behind the wheel, it was the performance and handling that were noticeably outstanding. Accelerating from 0-60mph in under 7 seconds put it on a par with the Porsche 928S and its top speed of 124mph would have been a great deal more had it a more slippery shape. What was even more impressive about this performance was the way it was delivered. Although one step removed from a rally car, the refinement of its gearbox and the low level of noise were extremely impressive.

The handling was quite superb and it would take a brave man to find the limits of its adhesion. With a 40/60 weight distribution, which changed to 44/56 with a passenger on board, plus 220/55VR Michelin TRXs on the front and smaller 190/55HRs on the back, the car could be thrown around in a manner that few others would allow. The driving position was good with the pedals positioned for heeling and toeing and the steering wheel perfectly placed.

The cabin itself was perhaps a little garish with the use of bright colours, but the strange looking seats were comfortable and held you securely. All the dials were there, but the trouble was that they tended to

The mid-engined Renault 5 Turbo was a successful rally-winning car out of which was developed a slightly modified version for sale to the general public. On only its third event, the car shot to stardom when it won the prestigious Monte Carlo rally (top picture).

get obscured by the steering wheel and were difficult to read in daylight.

Renault's rival, Peugeot, by the end of 1980 was in some trouble. Having already gained control of Citroen, they looked set to dominate not only the French motor industry but Europe's as well when they took over Chrysler's operation in Europe. It turned out though that Chrysler, subsequently renamed Talbot, became a real millstone around Peugeot's neck
. At the end of the '70s, Peugeot's reputation was largely based on one model, the 504. The manufacturer was perceived by most people as the maker of large cars, and with the recession in the car industry in full blast in 1980, it was one of the car maker's to suffer most. From a market share of 10.3% in France in 1978, it had plummeted to 6% in 1980, while as a group, it took 35% of the market compared to Renault's 43% Its share of the European market was also down to 15% from 17.5% and in the UK suffered a fall of one third of its sales in the same year. It was in dire trouble and there seemed every reason to believe that things would get worse for the group before it got better. Talbot's market share was also steadily decreasing in the important home French market to only 5% in mid 1981, down from 9% of a bigger market in 1979. The only hope for all 234 Talbot dealers was that the new baby car, the Samba, was coming by the end of 1981, and if early testing results were to be believed, would be a strong contender for Renault 5 sales. Where Peugeot/Talbot was better at making cars than Renault, though, they did not have the same marketing skills to exploit this advantage - but they were watching and learning.

With the purchase of Chrysler, Peugeot did acquire a couple of hot hatch models: the Sunbeam Lotus and Sunbeam 1600Ti.

The Sunbeam 1600ti was first seen at the Paris Show in September 1978 but was not available until the 1979 Geneva Show in March. Following in the footsteps of Ford, Chrysler decided that what they needed to improve the image of their range was a sportier version of a 'cooking' model, similar to what Ford had done with their Escort RS2000, Fiat with their Mirafiori Sport and Volkswagen with their Golf GTi.

What the Chrysler engineers did was basically take the largest engine they had, the 1598cc Avenger/Sunbeam unit, stick on a couple of twin-choke 40DCOE Weber carburettors, increase the compression, modify the camshaft and stick it into the

The Sunbeam 1600ti was introduced in April, 1979, but was never a great success.

Sunbeam bodyshell.

Although the horsepower was increased by 30bhp to 100bhp over the standard unit at 5800rpm, it was a fairly rough and ready way of producing a sporting car. The engine lacked refinement and although fine on the open road when it could be opened out, anything below 2500rpm and the car was inclined to stall.

It could reach a top speed of 107mph and a 0-60mph time of 10.7 secs. Where it failed, though, was in its poor economy, but by making a 1600 engine do the work of a 2 litre, a 17mpg return when driven hard was to be expected. More gentle driving, however, could see a return of 27mpg.

Its steering was pleasantly direct but the handling could be a little sensitive, mainly because of its live rear axle. Ironically, it sported a front air dam and rear spoiler which was noticeably missing from its more powerful Lotus-developed brother.

Where the 1600Ti scored was in its price. When introduced in 1979, it cost £3779, £370 less than the Renault 5 Gordini and £926 than the Golf GTi, but although it had virtually the same performance figures as these two cars, what was lacking was the overall refinement.

The Sunbeam Lotus was a car of a completely

EARLY DAYS

different character, and was more of a homologation special than anything else. Using the same idea as Ford, they enlisted the aid of an outside specialist in developing a car that could be the basis of a rally car. Where the Dagenham giant turned to Cosworth, the Coventry manufacturer looked East to Norfolk.

The part of Lotus was in developing the 2.2 litre, 16-valve engine and ZF five-speed gearbox. The bodyshell was taken off the now defunct assembly plant at Linwood in Scotland, where all Sunbeams were made, installed with stiffer suspension components, bigger anti-roll bar and stronger rear axle casing, and sent down to Hethel for its engine and gearbox.

The 2172cc unit actually started life as a 95.2 x 69.2mm, 1973cc engine, but a new crankshaft providing a longer stroke of 76.2mm resulted in the increased capacity. With a pair of twin-choke Dellorto fixed-choke carburettors, the engine produced 150bhp at 5750rpm with a maximum torque of

The Sunbeam Lotus was introduced in September, 1979. Again the model was made available to the public as it formed the basis of a competition model. As a rally car, it was highly successful, winning the Manufacturers' Title in 1981.

150lb/ft at 4500rpm. This enabled the car to rocket to 60mph in only 7.4 secs and reach a maximum speed of 121mph. With its pretty blunt shape, the performance took its toll on consumption. Driven hard the car only returned 12mpg and even gentler driven produced no better than 23mpg.

For sheer performance, the Sunbeam Lotus was top of the class, but it had rather curious handling. Grip on smooth roads was good but had a tendency to wander about at any speed. Ride was not particularly noteworthy and the steering was quite good, but since only 4500 examples were going to be made and sold for homologation purposes, Chrysler were pretty certain that there were enough performance-orientated enthusiasts around to sell them all.

Up until 1981, there were not any Golf GTi fighters either in the Italian or Japanese ranks, but car manufacturers from these countries were noticing the success of these hot hatches with more than a passing interest.

CHAPTER TWO

THE COMPETITION HOTS UP

Apart from pretenders to its crown, the Golf GTi was still the best hot hatchback by the end of 1981. Ford's XR3 was knocking on the door, and other manufacturers were looking ahead with great anticipation to producing their own version. Although the homologation specials were quicker, they either could not offer the all-round performance and refinement of VW or else were produced in too small numbers to make any impact.

For those customers in Germany who wanted to remain faithful to the Golf and yet still be able to accept the gauntlet thrown down by a passing special on the autobahn, they could avail themselves of the innumerable tuners who had sprung up around the country to attend to their needs. One such was Oettinger of Friedrichshafen which turned the standard 'tame' GTi into a 136bhp giant-killer. This 1600E/16 Golf was powered by a 16 valve 1.6 litre engine that would rev up to 8000rpm and accelerate from standstill to 60mph in under 7 seconds and go up to 125mph. It was the German answer, albeit not from the factory, to the Renault 5 Turbo.

Ever since it had been making cars, the Alfa Romeo name was synonymous with sporting cars, whether out-and-out sports racing cars or high performance saloons. Apart from a pedigree history of motor sport, it was the use of a twin-cam engine together with five-speed box that maintained their reputation.

The Alfasud, when introduced in 1971, was totally different. Not only was it made in Naples, the South of Italy, for political reasons, the car itself dispensed with the classic twin-cam configuration and used a flat-four boxer unit. Immediately, though, the model became a by-word for its legendary handling, and even after the Golf took its bow, it could still hold its own with the car from Wolfsburg as the Italian manufacturers had been careful to develop it continually. With the vogue for hatchbacks gaining momentum during the latter part of the 70's, what it needed was that third/fifth door.

A decade after its introduction the first hatchback models at last started to arrive. There were four models altogether, the 1.3 and 1.5 and the 1.3ti and 1.5ti. The single carburettor models, the 1.3 and 1.5, developed 79bhp and 84bhp respectively, while the twin carburettor 1.3 and 1.5ti versions developed 86bhp and 95bhp respectively.

It was in June, 1981, that the first hatchback Alfasuds arrived in Britain. Structural problems with the original body shell meant that the sill was quite high.

THE COMPETITION HOTS UP

The 1.5Ti was the top of the range hatchback when it was introduced. This was followed just over a year later by the 1.5 Cloverleaf 5-door hatch (below) 1.3SC and 1.5TiX.

Unfortunately the original design made it impossible for a rear door to be fitted that would stretch down to the floor - just by installing a frame around the rear door opening to maintain torsional stiffness, there was already a weight penalty of 1000lb. Since the brief to the engineers had been that the new model must retain its existing qualities, the handling remained as good as ever. Where it was let down slightly was in its use of 13 inch wheels.

In the 10 years since the car had been introduced there had been a great stride forward in tyres. The new generation of low profile 60 series tyres considerably increased the cornering power of any car as long as the suspension was properly set up. Where designers of new cars were able to take advantage of this fact and use 14 inch wheels and low profile tyres, Alfa Romeo were still stuck with the 13 inch wheels. It was when pushed to the limit that the car did not cling on as well as some of its more modern rivals might.

With regard to ride/handling the Alfasud still represented one of the best compromises available. It could take all but the roughest surfaces very well without suffering too much from roll or softness.

One of the criticisms of the car, only a small point but likely to become increasingly irritating after a while, was the location of the hatch opening lever. For some strange reason, on right-hand drive models, it remained located between the passenger seat and the door.

The very attractive, coupé-bodied hatchback Alfasud Sprint was designed by Giugiaro and introduced in August, 1977. The Sprint Veloce was the top of the range, although it took until 1980 to arrive. Powered by twin-choke carburettors, the engine developed 95bhp and the car was capable of 106mph. Its perky performance, coupled with marvellous handling and excellent torque, made this a gem of a car.

THE COMPETITION HOTS UP

As a basically old model, there was still enough dynamism in this car for Alfa Romeo to be able to offer it to the public and for potential customers to be attracted by it.

The mighty Fiat organisation also came up with their answer to the Golf GTi with two versions of the Strada: the 105TC and 125TC.

The Ritmo range was launched in Europe in 1978 and came to Britain a year later under the name of Strada. By 1980 it had become Europe's best selling car with over a million sold. The aerodynamic body was quite a contrast to Fiat's usual boxy style and laid emphasis on the Italian car maker's requirement of having a fast, relaxed cruiser. Originally introduced in Italy with a choice of three engine sizes, the 1100, 1300 and 1500, it would take until 1982 for a performance version to be offered.

Taking the 1600 twin overhead camshaft engine from the 132 and Supermirafiori models, they shoehorned it into the Strada frame, raised the compression to 9.3:1, fitted a twin-choke Weber carburettor, electronic ignition, larger clutch and radiator, utilised a five-speed gearbox, put its Pirelli P6's on alloy wheels, gave it larger brakes and introduced it as the Strada 105TC.

Changes to the engine took the power to 105bhp at 6100rpm and maximum torque to 98lb/ft at 4000rpm, giving it a top speed of 103mph and acceleration to 60mph in 10.4 secs. This was surprisingly slow because the growl from the engine and the look of the car made one feel that it was far faster than it actually was. Economy suffered slightly as the car was tuned for performance, but with an overall fuel consumption of 28mpg easily reached, it was not too expensive to run.

Although it revved sweetly, the engine was not as refined as the opposition, but it did have a lovely sound. Gearing in first and second allowed for a fair amount of wheelspin if undertaken with panache, and third was good for at least 70mph. The gearchange was a little sticky and took a little time to get used to mainly because the odd shape of the gear lever took some getting used to.

Roadholding, though, was superb aided by its low profile Pirellis. A fair amount of sensitivity was transmitted through the steering wheel which meant that while travelling rapidly on a winding road, the driver needed continuously to correct the direction. Although the traction was sensational, even on wet and slippery surfaces, hard cornering was difficult because the seats did not give enough lateral support to the driver. It would, however, only slide its front and rear ends at the driver's bidding. Ride was hard as the suspension was clearly sorted to hug the road, but there was not any trace of harshness.

Compared to the opposition, the Strada had a lot of character and was well equipped, but compared to the Golf GTi and others, it lacked the quality of finish and engineering, but despite it relative lack of performance, it was more of a fun car.

Interior of the Fiat Strada 105 Twin Cam was functional but pleasant and was an improvement over the original version.

The Fiat Strada 105TC was introduced into Britain in February, 1982, but following the re-styling of the Strada range the following year, was re-introduced in June 1983. To distinguish the new 105TC from its predecessor, the new model featured the new Fiat front-end symbol, a smooth bonnet without the air intakes and an uncluttered roof line.

Rather sadly, it was rather overshadowed with the introduction of the 125TC. Whereas it was clear that the Golf GTi was used by Fiat engineers as the benchmark in developing this higher powered model, when it finally came to the market, soon after the launch of the 105TC, the company's spokesmen made it clear that they regarded the new model, carrying Abarth decals, as more of a rival to the Porsche 924 and Alfa Romeo GTV. This was clearly marketing hype and was an attempt to explain away the somewhat higher price.

The 2 litre twin cam engine was prepared at Abarth's Corso Marche works in Turin and final assembly done at Fiat's Rivalta plant. The unit was the same as that used in the Mirafiori Sport 2000, Lancia Beta and Monte Carlo but the Abarth engineers had extracted 10bhp more with their modifications. Output was thus lifted to 125bhp at 5800rpm and torque to 125lb/ft at 3500rpm. Acceleration was better than the Golf with a 0-60mph time of 8.2sec and it reached 118mph flat out.

For the transmission Fiat supplied the casing, selectors and linkage which were assembled by ZF in West Germany. However gearchanging, while easy, lacked the efficiency of the Golf box, and in fourth and fifth gears tended to have an irritating whine.

On the road it handled well. The suspension was based on lessons learnt from Abarth's Group 2 racer. MacPherson struts were kept at the front and the negative offset geometry decreased the steering weight and fight and created better stability under braking.

Where the car scored over the Golf, though, was in the accommodation, especially in the back where there was a lot more room. The driver's position was comfortable with a comprehensive dash which contained red-calibrated instruments, but where the ergonomics were acceptable for all the other controls, they were not for the heating and ventilation. Through the rotary dials, it was impossible to get a warm feet/cool head situation, it had to be either one or the other.

THE COMPETITION HOTS UP

The Fiat Strada 125TC had the magic touch of Abarth but was only available in left-hand drive.

Altogether, the car had quite a lot going for it, with its performance perhaps being its strongest point, but, as Fiat only needed to produce 5000 units annually to conform to the requirements of motor sport's governing body, FISA, it was not worth their while to convert it to right-hand drive to bring the model to Britain.

By the beginning of 1982, Ford were introducing a fresh challenger into the hot hatchback market with the Fiesta XR2. They had already added go-faster stripes to one model and called it the S, and marketed in a limited way the 1.3 Supersport from January, 1981. The XR2, though, was a properly developed car.

The surprising thing about it initially was why had the old push-rod Kent engine been installed when the new 1.6 litre CVH would have fitted perfectly under the bonnet, a fact well known as many test examples had had the CVH installed. It was not an engineering problem either, as Ford's Special Vehicle Engineering department, under Rod Mansfield, were adept with these conversions. The answer lay within the Ford Motor Company. For the marketing men, it would have been a dilemma if the smaller, cheaper car out-performed the XR3.

The idea of a performance version of the Fiesta could be traced back to the '70s. American versions of the model, launched in 1976, utilised the 1.6 litre Kent engine which developed 66bhp. It was this unit which was developed by Ford into an amalgam of the Federal specification bottom end plus 1600GT engine cylinder head and camshaft and utilised by racer's in Ford's own Fiesta Championship. The engine was also used for more serious purposes, and Kent-engined Fiestas competed in the 1979 and 1980 Monte Carlo rallies.

When it finally appeared in December 1981, the XR2 was well received. It met Rod Mansfield's targets of being the fastest production Fiesta, topped 100mph by 4mph and went from standstill to 60mph in 9.4sec. Breathing through twin Webers, the engine developed 84bhp at 5500rpm and 91lb/ft torque at 2800rpm.

The precision of its steering was its most noticeable attribute and it was pleasant to use - light when parking but keeping plenty of feel at speed. Using the stronger Escort gearbox equipped with standard 1.6 ratios, changing gear was also a delight, although the ratios necessitated constant shifting into third when travelling in fourth over a hilly route. What the car missed at this stage, though, was that fifth gear which was also lacking on the XR3.

Averaging nearly 29mpg, the car was tolerably economical, however its small 7.5 gallon fuel tank meant that on average a refill was necessary before 200 miles had passed, and filling the tank up to the brim was a long drawn-out process.

Ventilated front discs were fitted on the front and drums on the rear, and although better than fitted onto earlier models, the driver needed to push his left leg down hard to stop quickly. This, however, was more due to the pedal than the brakes themselves, this fault being remedied by Ford later on.

When pressed hard around corners, the car understeered, but did so in a safe fashion and kept on the line and did not roll or pitch. The firm spring rates were those used on the Fiesta S and gave a lively ride especially over rough surfaces.

Sitting in the driving seat the most noticeable thing was how offset the steering wheel was which allowed an unobstructed view of the dials - the speedometer and rev counter flanking the water temperature and fuel guages.

Comfort in the car was high with an excellent driving position, well placed pedals and tight fitting Recaro bucket seats giving good lumbar, shoulder and lateral support. For this reason the XR2 was one of the most satisfying cars to drive hard.

Although the XR2 could not offer a very high top speed, it was the marvellous mid-range performance, chuckability and mechanical refinement that made it such an attractive car. Against the Alfasud 1.5 Hatchback, it was £700 more expensive and £174 more than the Renault 5 Gordini, but with its clever decals and muscular stance, the XR2 exuded a macho image that was enough to influence many into buying it.

The XR2, when it appeared in December, 1981, was a sporting version of the Fiesta range (above). The 1.6 Kent-engined Fiesta that was entered in both the 1979 (below) and 1980 Monte-Carlo rallies, and the Ford-backed Fiesta Championship, were major influences in XR2 production.

THE COMPETITION HOTS UP

It was in late 1980 that Austin-Rover proudly announced the Metro. Although a familiar shape now, at the time it was completely individual, not likely to be confused with any rivals, and yet still good looking.

In the five model line-up that was announced, what was obviously missing was a sporting version, but such were the sales expectations, Austin-Rover felt that the range did not need a performance model to boost sales, and rather than concentrate on catering to a small segment in this small car class, it was better to pump out as many standard models as they could.

As the model used the old A series engine it did not take long for specialist tuners to start modifying it, and when John Cooper's name began to be associated with a performance version of the model, expectations soared seeing what he had done to the little Mini in the 60's in creating the Mini-Cooper and Mini-Cooper S. Unfortunately, Austin-Rover had other ideas about the project and so it never reached mass production stage.

The MG Metro was introduced in May, 1982, and in four and a half years saw only cosmetic changes.

When the market had settled down again after the introduction of the Metro, it was time to stimulate interest again. Austin-Rover had been carrying out their own market research into a sportier performing vehicle, and every indication was that there was some demand. It was important for the name to be right, and further market research showed that the MG name was just right for the job.

To call it a performance car would be wrong, for it patently was not. 100mph could be coaxed from it, and a 0-60mph time of 12.2 secs achieved, but although it was made to look macho and quick, Austin-Rover's policy with the model was specifically to keep it from flying for insurance reasons. At a time when they were scrabbling for every sale they could get in an effort to keep their market share, and even get it back again to the psychologically important 20 per cent level, a low insurance rating would be a useful asset in the battle of the super-minis.

The 1275cc engine was developed to produce 72bhp at 6000rpm and peak torque of 73lb/ft at 4000rpm. The compression ratio was also raised from the standard car's 9.4:1 to 10.5:1. Outwardly, the car was very similar to the normal Metro except that its wider 155/70SR12 Dunlop SP4s were put on alloy wheels.

It was never in the same class as the XR2 or Alfa Hatchback, but where it really scored over its rivals was in its cheaper running costs and good looks.

Whether Austin-Rover could really justify the expense and effort put into turbocharging the MG Metro considering the potential sales it was likely to have was never really to the point. The October Motor Show was coming up and Austin-Rover had to be seen to be doing something. At that time, their cupboard was a little bare of new models and

Announced at the 1982 British Motor Show, the MG Metro Turbo added a high performance dimension to the Austin Rover range of small cars.

THE COMPETITION HOTS UP

lopsided in its offerings. At the lower level were the Mini, Metro and, to some extent, Acclaim while at the other end were the Ambassador and Rover. With the demise of the dumpy Allegro and Maxi, it was the Ital, born as the Marina the previous decade, which was holding the middle ground. Austin-Rover needed not only to turn attention away from this, but also capture as much of the spotlight as possible in preparation for the arrival of the Maestro in 1983.

In fact, the engineering effort was hardly excessive with regard to the Turbo. Because the venerable A series engine was not cross-flow, like so many of its modern contemporaries, the turbo installation could be kept simple. Also, by getting Lotus to provide the development, they not only got the state of the art turbocharging knowledge applied, but also got it cheaper than if they had done it in-house.

The main turbo components were simple and well-tried. The Garrett T3 turbocharger was placed under the ARG - nee SU - carburettor and blew through it. Compression ratio of the engine was the standard 1300's 9.4:1 rather than the 10:5 of the naturally aspirated MG. This was still very high for a turbo but provided good low speed pull. It was the use of the part-electronic turbo control system that was the one innovation on the car which smoothed the turbo power delivery and kept it out of trouble. But that was not all. By fooling the diaphragm, through a system of links, it managed to bridge the gap between the often dead bottom end of the power curve and quickly accelerating mid to upper end so often found on other turbo cars. The basic control was a wastegate which was set to blow off at only 4.psi, a very low figure by most standards. However, above 4000rpm, the electronics held the wastegate closed longer, working to a pre-determined curve which took account of the need to stay clear of the knock zone while still giving boost up to 7.5psi.

At a glance, the underbonnet view of the MG Metro Turbo looked very similar to that of the standard MG Metro down to the ribbed, polished alloy rocker with its red oil filler cap and MG octagon badge and even red ignition plug tension leads. Yet an extra 21bhp was squeezed from the A-plus engine by means of the Garrett AiResearch T3 turbocharger hidden between the engine and the bulkhead, the rotor spinning up to 120,000rpm. The turbocharger boosted power output to 93bhp at 6130rpm and torque to 85lb/ft at 2650rpm.

The MG Metro and Metro Turbo, outwardly similar, but differed in detail as the turbocharged car had much higher performance levels.

THE COMPETITION HOTS UP

A side window demisting system was exclusive to the MG Metro Turbo as was the speedometer which was marked up to 130mph instead of 110mph, and the tachometer was red lined at 7000rpm. A LED boost gauge in the tachometer displaced the digital clock which was moved to the centre of the facia. The most obvious change, however, was a change in the main interior colour from black to grey mixed with the same red as found in the MG Metro. The red piping across the door trim, however, was unique to the Turbo.

Power output was a modest 93bhp at 6130rpm, but the figure which deserved more attention was the torque peak of 85lb/ft at a low 2650rpm. The secret of the electronic system was that the boost pressure was modulated to stay very close to this figure for much of the way to 5500rpm.

This kind of output placed new demands on the A series bottom end, which in its standard form was not renowned for its tolerance of high loadings so it was modified with strengthened pistons, enlarged big end bearing caps and a nitrided forged crankshaft.

The money spent by Austin Rover on the turbo side, and especially on the electronic control, was not going to be wasted since clearly it was going to find other applications in the Austin-Rover range. But where real money should have been spent, on the transmission, it was not forthcoming. It was this aspect of the car that was the most displeasing thing about it. Where it accelerated strongly up the gears to the 7000rpm red line, a fifth gear was clearly missing.

Thus the suspension set-up, which provided such tremendous roadholding and predictable and safe steering, good brakes, and a car which was such fun to drive, was completely spoilt. All that was done was to raise the final drive ratio, the new 3.21:1 unit giving 18.6mph per 1000rpm in top gear. That meant the MG Turbo was pulling almost exactly 6000 rpm at its 110mph maximum and was able to accelerate from 0-60mph in 9.9 seconds.

This small performance machine was approximately £250 more expensive that the XR2 and £450 less than the XR3i, so did not quite fit in anywhere. Compared to the Fords, its stated opposition at the time of its launch, it did lack mechanical refinement and chassis finesse but its superb driveability and safe feel to it compensated to some extent for these shortcomings.

Earlier in the year, Renault had introduced a turbocharger on the 5 Gordini. It was not a question of simply bolting on a turbocharger. Discs were now fitted to all wheels, light alloy wheels with 5.5 inch rims became standard and stiffer springs and anti-roll bars front and rear were now fitted. It was a great improvement over its predecessor, its turbocharger doing away with the thrashiness of the engine and consequent high noise level when at speed. While not a road burner, it was a high performing small car that delivered its punch in such a relaxed manner that journey times could be reduced without seemingly trying. The new model was a little more expensive, but its top speed of 112mph and a 0-60mph figure of 9.8sec was comparable to that of the Golf GTi. It was priced in the UK at £5,752 compared to the £5,750 of the XR3 and £6176 of the Golf GTi.

Reaping further benefits from its vast experience of turbocharging in motor sport, the Renault 5 Gordini Turbo was introduced in France in September, 1981, and in Britain in May, 1982 (overleaf). While still using the 4 cylinder 1397cc engine, the Turbo was 18 per cent more powerful than the original 5 Gordini, but that was only one side of its character, for it became outstandingly flexible and easy to drive around town thanks to a gain of almost 30 per cent in torque which went up from 81.4 to 108.5lb/ft at 4000rpm. The 5 Gordini Turbo was the fourth Renault production model to be turbocharged and followed the 5 Turbo (road-going and competition versions), the 18 Turbo and the 30 Diesel Turbo.

THE COMPETITION HOTS UP

The mid-engined, rear-wheel drive Renault 5 Turbo was the spearhead of Renault's rallying programme, but it was never marketed in Britain.

THE COMPETITION HOTS UP

The Innocenti de Tomaso with its all-plastic bumpers and lift-up back.

Although never marketed in the United Kingdom, it was from Italy that one of the finest small cars was produced that showed Austin Rover how they should have tackled putting the pep into the normally aspirated Metro.

It was always regarded as bit of a blunder when British Leyland sold off to the Italian government their Italian car making company - Innocenti. This in turn was bought by Alessandro de Tomaso, already owner of Maserati, who then proceeded to turn to his engineers for their version of a small, sporty car.

The result was a delightfully small, yet spacious car, that delivered the power from its three potted Dahaitsu engine in a gracious and smooth fashion. Such was the work on this engine that it pushed the little company to the forefront of three cylinder expertise. Its 993cc developed 52bhp at 5600rpm with maximum torque of 55lb ft at 3200rpm.

In France, Citroen launched the Visa GT mid-1982 in place of the unsuccessful Visa Super X. The new model replaced the 1219cc 64bhp engine of the Super X with a 1360cc unit delivering 80bhp. Top speed was 105mph, instead of the Super X's 97mph and the GT used less petrol. With this version, Citroen were aiming at young drivers and were trying to nibble at the 10-year old Renault 5, still number one in France, but losing ground.

For once, Citroen appeared to be following motoring fashion rather than originating it having spotted the impressive growth in the small hatchback performance car market. Where it was the odd man out was that it had four doors in what was otherwise a strictly coupe market.

The Citroen Visa GT was one of the first hatchbacks to feature a rear spoiler.

One of the first of the Japanese manufacturers to offer a hot hatchback was Mitsubishi. They had fitted turbochargers to many cars in their range, such as to the Sapporo, Galant and Lancer, and so it was not surprising when they turned their attention to the 1400 GLX Hatchback first seen in Britain at the 1978 Motor Show in Birmingham.

The turbocharger was downstream of the carburettor with precautionary controls installed into the system to prevent over-boosting. The power output was pushed up to 103.5bhp at 5000rpm and a maximum torque of 114lb/ft at 3500rpm giving the car a top speed of 105mph and a 0-60mph time of 9.9 secs.

Drive was through the two front wheels via the unique four-speed x 2 manual transmission as on the standard 1400 which offered a choice of four gears for both power and economy. The final drive was 3.47:1 and the clutch was larger.

The punch of the turbocharger was felt at higher speeds at a time when the standard 1400's performance would have been beginning to struggle, but to get the most out of it, it was necessary to keep the right foot hard down to keep the turbo spinning on boost, but the 41.2 secs it took to reach 100mph really showed the benefit of the turbocharger.

In the lower range of gears, the car accelerated well right up to the 6000rpm rev limit. In fourth gear, the car would reach 105mph before the rev limiter would cut-in to safeguard against over-revving. In the higher range of gears, maximum speed was reached at a more subdued 4600rpm.

Mid-range punch was good in the lower gear range, and response felt between 60 to 80mph was as impressive as it was between 20 to 40mph and was a vast improvement over the standard model's.

In having eight gear ratios, fuel consumption should have been better than 29mpg, but working the turbocharger hard had to be paid for.

The Mirage did not have any particular bad habits, understeer being negligible and the car responding very well to the steering in a corner. The good handling, though, was at the expense of ride which was a little harsh. The all-independent suspension was much firmer than the standard 1400's and while alright over smoother surfaces, produced sharp vertical movements when traversing rougher surfaces.

Just £200 cheaper than the Golf GTi when it appeared in the summer of 1982, the 1400 GLX Hatchback Turbo was still more expensive than any other comparable car. Its performance was not quite in the same league as the Metro Turbo or Renault 5 Gordini Turbo, but on longer journeys, it would be much less tiring because of its less fussy transmission.

Altogether it was a thoroughly well-built car that had overall merit and no specific vices, but compared to its major rivals, it lacked charisma, which is something that cannot be easily built into a car.

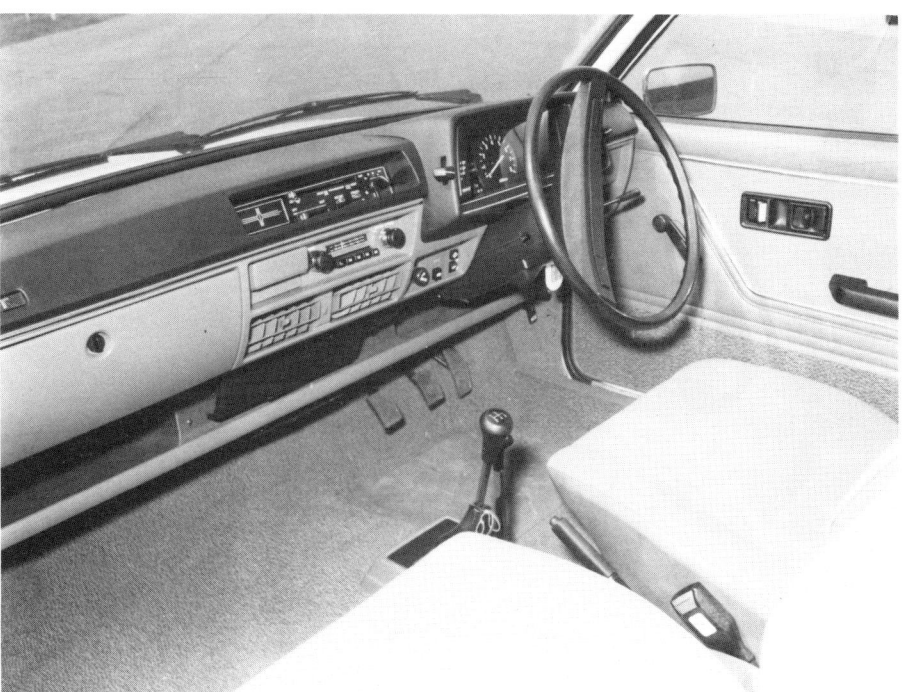

The interior of the Colt showing the "super-shift" gear lever which altered the rear axle ratio to give either performance or economy. Selection could be made in any gear by depressing the clutch pedal.

THE COMPETITION HOTS UP

The Golf GTi still ruled supreme despite the extra competition it faced.

CHAPTER THREE

THE STAKES ARE RAISED

So often was the Golf GTi mentioned as the yardstick against which other speedy hatchbacks should be judged, that it became almost boring, but it was so right in so many respects that Volkswagen were able to sit back and watch the deutschmarks come rolling in. Other cars bettered some aspects of the Golf, but none managed to beat it consistently in all departments. Only Ford came really close with the extra bouncy Escort, the XR3.

Then Volkswagen raised the stakes with the 1.8 litre GTi, announced in Germany in August 1982. The intention was not really to increase the power, this, they felt, was adequate enough, but to give the model a more flexible and quieter powerplant. The unit itself was not one specially made for the Golf, but was an off-the-shelf job that was modified far beyond the carb-fed 75bhp 1.8 four that went into the most basic Audi coupe. In the hands of Peter Hofbauer, it was transformed into a smooth and responsive engine that not only equalled its predecessor's maximum power output but also boasted a much flatter torque curve.

The new powerplant was just as compact but marginally lighter than the 1.6 litre. It also had lighter pistons, longer conrods, which theoretically helped to reduce friction, and a better balanced lightweight camshaft. Together with a revised camshaft profile and bigger diameter intake and exhaust valves, these modifications resulted in a different engine characteristic with the emphasis on flexibility rather than on high revs.

With a high compression ratio of 10:1, and a higher final drive ratio the revised 1.8 litre unit developed 112bhp at 5800rpm instead of 110bhp at 6100rpm. While the outgoing engine delivered a maximum torque of 101lb/ft at a very high 5000rpm, the torque curve of the '83 model powerplant was 111lb/ft at 3500rpm.

These figures suggest that the new GTi engine was beefier and less nervous than its predecessor. There was not much between old and new at the top end of the rev band - the 1.8 litre topped out at 113mph, so it was only 5.0mph faster than the 1.6, but between 2000 and 5000rpm, the bigger engine felt decidedly more competent and lost none of its much acclaimed urgent throttle response. Whereas the 1600cc engine called for 5000rpm or more to carry enough torque into the next gear, the new powerplant allowed you to change up at around 4000rpm and still accelerate briskly if desired.

The Golf GTi still retained its muscular stance right up to the Mark II shape.

Returning an average of almost 29mpg, the larger engined Golf was more frugal than its predecessor. 40mpg was within the bounds of possibility if the car was not driven too hard, but such unmitigating fun was it to drive, that this figure was not realistically feasible.

Accelerating up through the gears was pure delight, the ratios second to none and very close. 0-60mph could be reached in 8.3 secs and a top speed of 113mph taking almost 43 secs.

Although the ride was on the stiff side, the suspension was more of a compromise than many other of its rivals, but to turn it into a roadholding leech, Bilstein offered a 'Sportspaket' suspension kit that also included 60 series tyres instead of the 70 series Cinturatos.

The interior was very functional, but the seats were very comfortable. Vision, however, although good to the front and sides, was spoilt to the rear because of the unfashionably wide rear pillars

There was no doubt that this definitive high performance hatchback was now in another class as far as all other rivals were concerned, only the Ford Escort XR3 coming close to it, but even that had to give best to it in most departments.

VW tried to repeat the success of the Golf GTi in a different class with the new Polo Coupe. The newcomer featured most of the GTi's cosmetic touches with mildly flared wings, low section tyres, red coachlining framing the grille and matt black rear window surround.

However its 1.3 litre engine developed only 75bhp maximum power at 5800rpm and a maximum torque of 75lb/ft at 3600rpm, and although it was more elegant and sporty than the standard square-back Polo, it never came to the fore like its GTi brother. The Polo GT was too heavily tarted up to pass as a subtle Q-car, but contrary to some of its apparently equally potent class rivals, the performance of the little VW did match its looks as it was able to sprint from 0-60mph in 11.5 secs and reach a top speed of 104mph.

The VW Polo Coupé S with GTi Engineering body styling kit.

THE STAKES ARE RAISED

Ford's second attempt at producing a high performance version of their Escort was the XR3i introduced in October, 1982 and for the first time, refinement was clearly detectable.

The XR3i, successor to the XR3, was continually uprated by Ford so that later models were themselves superior to earlier ones.

The 1.6 engine was fed by Bosch K-Jetronic fuel injection and delivered 105bhp at 6000rpm and 101lb/ft torque at 4800rpm. The front seats were well shaped to provide all the support for fast driving, their covering matching that of the door panel inserts.

THE STAKES ARE RAISED

The original XR3 did a tolerable job, but although it needed better ride and handling, Ford denied there was anything seriously wrong with it while at the same time admitting there was a problem by carrying out a series of suspension modifications. Their alterations, however, did not improve the ride quality, they merely changed it. Then they handed the car over to their Special Vehicle Engineering group and at last real progress was made. SVE not only tackled the ride problem but also gave the 1.6 litre engine injection for smoothness, more power and greater fuel economy.

The Bosch K-Jetronic fuel injected 1600 XR3 specification engine now gave 105bhp at 6000rpm and 101lb/ft torque at 4800rpm and took on a more purposeful air which was missing from the earlier carburettored model. The five-speed box was slick and had well chosen ratios. The maxima in the gears were 31, 52, 77 and 104. It reached 60mph from standstill half a second quicker than the XR3, taking 8.6 secs. and could reach a maximum of 116mph, 3mph quicker than the Golf's top speed.

Handling was now superb, the steering was excellent, ride was better and the brakes were improved, but road noise was high and did not quite match the Golf in that department. It did score over the Golf inside, an area where Ford were traditionally good, and was comfortable and well thought out. The final result was a great success and in every way the XR3i was in the same category as its traditional and sworn enemy - the new Golf GTi, and being a little cheaper, £6,278 against that of £6500 for the Golf, it repre-

The downforce generated by the XR3i's spoiler helped high-speed stability.

sented the only real rival to the car from Wolfsburg apart from the special Escort RS1600i which was introduced at the same time. Since this model was a homologation special of which only 5000 examples were produced to comply with FIA Group A homologation, it was not really in the same category as the other two models.

Compared to its brother, its fuel injected engine had 10 more horses to play with, and while displaying a lack of ride comfort, the steering, damping and tyres were as good as SVE's version. Chief chassis engineer Otto Stulle had revised the front suspension and relocated the rear shock absorber mounts while adjustable dampers successfully reduced bump steer and the tail's tendency to weave about. It was shod with 15-inch wheels, larger than the XR3's, fitted with ultra-low profile Dunlop 195/50VR15 D4tyres, thereby putting more rubber on the ground. It was also fitted with a much deeper front spoiler and a two tier rear wing.

Under the bonnet the RS1600i also received the Bosch K-Jetronic fuel injected 1.6 litre engine, the same as used in the XR3i. Along with an uprated camshaft and a modified cylinder head, the power was increased by 10bhp to 115bhp at 6000rpm. This allowed a top speed of 116mph and a 0-60mph in 8.7sec, almost identical to those of the XR3i.

The RS1600i was a development of the Escort for competition purposes. Work was carried out at Cologne in Germany instead of Special Vehicle Engineering near Brentwood, but the end result was not much different from the standard XR3i. Produced in limited numbers and bearing the renowned 'RS' prefix, it earned for itself a certain kudos.

THE STAKES ARE RAISED

The Astra GTE, Vauxhall's answer to the Golf.

General Motors' answer to the GTi came rather late in the day. As far as sheer performance was concerned, the sporty Opel Kadett/Vauxhall Astra had in the past always come off second best against its hottest rivals, the VW Golf GTi and the XR3i. The Kadett's 90bhp 1.6 litre carb-fed four was even more easily outranked by the GTi's modified 1.8 litre fuel-injected 112bhp powerplant and by the Escort's new 105bhp injection engine. Opel hit back, though, with a much more fearsome competitor powered by the potent 1.8 engine from the Cavalier CD/SRi and was first shown at the 1983 Geneva Show.

The Vauxhall Astra 1600S was added to the range in September, 1982.

The Vauxhall Astra SR was powered by a 90bhp 1.6 litre engine with crossflow alloy head and overhead camshaft. This transverse-mounted power-unit drove the front wheels through a completely new wide ratio 5-speed gearbox with overdrive 4th and 5th gears, for relaxed high speed travel and outstanding fuel economy.

The Astra SR had a striking, purposeful appearance. It was immediately recognisable by its all black grille, black painted accents, and the distinctive deep front spoiler, ABS wheel arch extensions and black plastic side spoilers between the wheel arches. Roadholding of the Astra was already recognised as outstanding, but this was enhanced on the SR by wide 5½J × 14 inch alloy wheels and low profile 185/60 tyres.

The Astra SR replaced the Opel Kadett SR in Britain with which it compared closely in sporty styling and interior appointments.

Astra SR, like other models in the Astra range, was developed as a result of extensive wind tunnel testing. It had the typical Vauxhall wedge shaped design - a raked grille with integrated front spoiler, sloping bonnet merging gradually into the line of the windscreen and a carefully shaped spoiler where the roof line joined the slope of the rear end. In practical terms, this meant lower fuel consumption. In addition, aerodynamic lift forces at either end of the car were minimal and cross-wind stability was of a very high order.

The driver quickly felt at home behind the wheel in the Recaro seats. Switches were easily reached and clearly marked. They were arranged so that the controls for the primary functions - those directly connected with driving - were arranged close to the rim of the steering wheel including the turn

THE STAKES ARE RAISED

indicator, horn, headlamp flasher and dimmer, windscreen washer and wipers.

The interior heater used the mixed air principle, providing precise and rapid adjustment of the temperature. A two-speed tangential fan was quiet in operation and provided good air circulation. Two vents in the instrument panel were independently adjustable for direction and flow. Two further vents kept the side windows free from condensation.

The Astra SR had a remarkably low noise level achieved in a number of different ways. The engine itself was inherently quiet and the body largely free from wind noise. In addition, chassis vibrations were filtered out by means of the principle of the uncoupled floor pan, taken from the Carlton, Senator and Monza. Here, the rocker panels, or lower body sills, were no longer part of the floor pan, but were welded to it to damp out vibration.

The 1.6 litre 90bhp engine had an aluminium cylinder head designed on the cross-flow principle for better fuel charge distribution. A separate housing for the overhead camshaft reduced noise and allowed dismantling of the camshaft without removing the cylinder head. Hydraulic valve lifters, a standard feature in Vauxhall and Opel engines for many years, eliminated tappet noise and the need for routine valve clearance adjustment.

The deep skirted, ribbed cast iron cylinder block was fitted with a five bearing crankshaft with counterweights to cut down engine vibration and noise. An electric engine fan operated only when necessary, reducing noise and power drain as well as saving fuel. The aluminium cross-flow radiator had a nylon expansion reservoir so that the coolant level can be easily checked and replenished without removing the radiator cap.

The 1.6 litre engine developed 90bhp at 5800rpm and had a 9.2 to 1 compression ratio. It was almost 'square' with a bore of 80mm and a stroke of 79.5mm.

The front wheel suspension of the Astra employed the proven MacPherson principle and by means of careful geometry outstanding manoeuvrability and stability was achieved. Steering was by rack and pinion.

The wide track of the Astra SR provided maximum comfort, together with safe, neutral driving characteristics free from excessive self-centring action.

Against the Golf GTi and Escort XR3, the Astra SR lacked overall power and did not quite win for Vauxhall the cache they sought, and eventually found, with the GTE.

A new range of models, with distinctive two-tone body finish and with an array of special equipment, were added to the Vauxhall Astra series in May 1982. The Vauxhall Astra EXP range, produced in limited numbers, included EXP 1.3 litre 3- and 5-door hatchbacks, an Astra EXP 1.6 litre 5-door hatchback and a sporty Astra EXP "S" 1.6 litre 3-door hatchback.

The three EXP models were finished in black above the waistline and below the bumpers and side rubbing strips, with contrasting antique gold metallic paintwork between. An alternative choice of finish was hazel brown above and below the middle band of antique gold. The central colour was outlined by a pin stripe at waist level and 'strobe' striping above the side rubbing strips.

The wheels of the EXP models were finished in antique gold with black wheel hubs. A removable transparent sun roof was fitted, the windscreen was laminated and the windows were tinted. Two front fog lamps, rear window wash/wipe system, a remote control driver's door mirror and a mirror on the passenger's door, were provided.

Inside, the EXP models were finished in beige velour. The door trims were carpeted at the lower edge and the vinyl door panels extended right up to the window. A cigar lighter was standard. Automatic transmission was available on the two 5-door models.

The EXP "S" sports model was finished in Carmine Red on the upper part of the body with matt black paintwork below the bumpers.

In place of the gold painted steel wheels of the EXP, it was fitted with wide 5½J 14 inch light alloy wheels with 185/60 steel braced extra low profile radial tyres. Front and rear spoilers and wheel arch extensions added to the sports appearance of the EXP "S".

The EXP 'S' 1.6 litre version of the hatchback was a first tentative step by General Motors towards producing a sports version of the Astra. Encouraged by the results, they then produced the Astra S and GTE.

THE STAKES ARE RAISED

The 1.8 litre, fuel injected engine of the Astra GTE.

The excellent four cylinder in the new GTE boasted a chain-driven overhead camshaft, hydraulic tappets, electronic breakerless ignition system, a light-alloy cross-flow cylinder head and the latest version of the Bosch LE Jetronic fuel injection with an in-built fuel-feed cut-off device which reduced the fuel consumption under trailing throttle. Developing 115bhp at 5800rpm and a torque of 111lb/ft at a high 4800rpm the 2175lb sports hatch could sprint in 9.2sec from 0 to 60mph and reach a maximum speed of 116mph. That made it slower to 60mph than a GTi with its superior power to weight ratio and sprint gearing, but a winner in top speed.

Together with the new engine the Kadett/Astra GTE also received some cosmetic change, improvements to the interior, such as a pair of excellent Recaro front seats, and revised suspension and the drivetrain. To reduce drag and give the car a distinctly sporty appearance, there were front and rear spoilers complemented by flared wheel arches, aerodynamically shaped door mirrors, sill extensions and flush alloy wheels fitted with 185/60HR-14 low-profile tyres.

On the road, the GTE possessed fine handling and ride, good brakes and marvellous mechanical refinement, but where it fell down slightly against the

Ford and Volkswagen was in its delivery of mid-range performance, more due to its high gearing than anything else.

Until the arrival of the new look Golf GTi in September, 1983, the GTE proved to be superior to its two tough rivals in most respects - but in some it beat them only by a whisker. The dressed up Astra/Kadett was marginally faster in top speed, was significantly more comfortable, better equipped and, above all, considerably roomier than its other challengers in the class.

In the UK it was priced at £6412, nearly £400 cheaper than the GTi but was more expensive than the XR3i at £6151. According to official steady-speed figures, it was also the most economical of the trio, nudging 50mpg at 56mph, and over 37mpg at 75mph due mostly to better aerodynamics. Much higher gearing (23.5mph/1000rpm in fifth) also gave the GTE a long-striding cruising gait that neither the Ford nor the fussier VW could match.

The Nova was introduced in April, 1983, with the SR, the sporty version, going on sale the following July. It was powered by a new version of the 1297cc overhead camshaft unit used in the Astra and Cavalier. Equipped with an alloy cross-flow head, electronic ignition and hydraulic valve lifters for minimal maintenance, the engine developed 70bhp at 5800rpm and 74.5lb/ft of torque at 3800rpm which gave the car a top speed of 96mph and a 0–60mph acceleration figure of 11.7 secs. It drove through a five-speed gearbox with overdrive fourth and fifth gears for maximum fuel economy, low wear and quiet performance at high speeds.

THE STAKES ARE RAISED

The Peugeot 205GT was the quickest of the five-door 205s. The 1360cc engine had twin carburettors and developed 80bhp. It was mated to of 106mph while showing a return of above 50mpg at a constant 56mph. Externally the car was restrained with only a rear spoiler, a bodysid

ive-speed gearbox that was designed to give good performance rather than a very high gear for cruising. The result was a car that was capable
ape scheme and alloy wheels to give the game away.

THE STAKES ARE RAISED

The coming of spring in 1983 brought with it a fresh aggressive image for Peugeot. Within a matter of weeks, the marque launched the 305GT, the 505 petrol turbo and the 205. To boot, they unveiled on the same day as the 205, the 205 R16 (16 for 16 valves) a mid-engined, four-wheel-drive rally car, that was due to make its competition debut in 1984. The 205 hatchback was the most important of them all and had as its target the 10 year old Renault 5 range. Up until this time, the remarkable 5 had maintained a 13 per cent share of the French market and had succeeded in fending off every attack, French or foreign. The 205, though, looked from the start like giving it a run for its money.

It seemed odd that such a quiet, respectable company like Peugeot should produce a small car so eye-catchingly good looking as the 205, with its gracefully plunging bonnet. Very soon it was not only catching the eyes, but also the customers bringing in more than 1000 orders a day during the first weeks of its life.

One interesting point was that the top-of-the-range 205GT (80bhp, 106mph) was attracting 15 per cent of the sales, and not 10 per cent as forecast by the marketing men. The advent of the 205GTi, though, was still a year away.

The Talbot Samba S was a sporting, three-door addition to the Samba range. It was powered by the 1360cc engine which in this car developed 79 bhp at 5800rpm which enabled it to reach a top speed of 104mph and 0–62mph in 11.7 secs. Transmission was via a five-speed gearbox. The Samba S gained a spoiler, a rear anti-roll bar, servo assisted brakes and 165×70×13 low profile tyres. The model did not last long, though, and was phased out in October, 1984, just two years after its introduction.

The Peugeot 104ZS was startlingly short and looked as though a designer's knife had been taken to its back.

The 205 range reached British showrooms in the autumn of 1983 where it replaced the forgotten 104, of which the ZS model was the fastest. This was a short hatchback, longer than a Mini by no more than 12 inches. The 66bhp engine that was in the model when it first appeared in British showrooms in 1975 was replaced by the 1360cc Douvrin Renault Peugeot unit that produced 72bhp at 6000rpm and a maximum torque of 79lb/ft at 3000rpm. Translated into performance terms, the car had a top speed of 96mph and a 0-60mph time of 11.8 secs. The acceleration times were aided not only by the light weight of the car (1932lbs) but also by its excellent gear change. With a fuel tank holding 8.8 gallons and returning a mpg figure of 36, it had a useful range of over 300 miles.

Its looks were deceptive for it could still accommodate quite a large amount of luggage.

THE STAKES ARE RAISED

At the time, the 104ZS was a late 70's counterpart to the Mini-Cooper, the nearest rival to it being the Renault 5 Gordini, which was faster and accelerated more quickly, but was £1,300 more to buy and more costly to run, but it never really caught the public imagination, and very few were to be found certainly on British roads.

In April 1983 Lancia started to bring into Britain their revised Delta range, which included a 1600GT that carried forward a company tradition, since it was they who had pioneered the gran turismo concept with the 1950s Aurelias.

Having said that, it had to be conceded that Deltas were slightly up-market derivations of Fiat Stradas, sharing almost identical mechanisms beneath a different shell, styled by Guigiaro, so the 1600's engine was the familar 105bhp twin-cam as found in Stradas and Mirafioris, plus Lancia Betas, Trevis and Prismas (from June). But with a top speed of only 100mph and taking 14sec from 0 to 60mph, it was not yet Lancia's entry into the hot hatchback market.

It was in the September 1983 that Lancia launched what they said was the world's fastest 1600cc car - and in so doing presented the Golf GTi with its strongest ever Italian rival. Thanks to a turbocharged version of the venerable but lusty 1585cc twin-cam engine, the new model - the Delta HF - was capable of 122mph. And that made it not only the quickest 1.6 litre around but also faster than any other small hotshoe sports saloon currently on the market and put it in a class above such vehicles as the Golf, Escort and Astra.

A Garrett AiResearch T3 turbocharger was fitted to the transversely mounted engine along with an air-to-air intercooler, with a maximum boost pressure of 10psi, a Microplex electronic ignition system which had a micro-processor, and a twin-choke 32DAT Weber. The blower did help give a significant increase in power from 105bhp for the normal GT1600 to 130bhp at 5600rpm. The torque increase was even more significant up from 99lb/ft to 140 at 3700rpm.

Apart from the turbo addition, the Delta Turbo (which saw the return of the sporty HF designation, last used on the rally winning Fulvia back in the early '70s) got numerous engine modifications such as sodium exhaust valves, an oil-cooling radiator and lowered compression ratio.

The Lancia technicians had also been at work outside the engine bay. The springs were stiffer both at the front (by 13 per cent) and rear (by 8 per cent) and the dampers revised. The steering benefitted from a slight alteration to the rack and pinion geometry.

There were few exterior changes compared with the GT. Plastic side skirts were painted black as was some of the trim. There were also two black bonnet ducts to improve under-bonnet cooling.

The engine was far from quiet but road noise was well insulated. On the move straight-line stability was excellent with an impressive ride and well-balanced handling with impeccable manners. There was a natural tendency to understeer which became oversteer on the limit. The all-disc brakes, however, gave the driver a good sense of security.

The Lancia Delta model range never caught on in England. The turbo version, though, was a fine driver's car.

When introduced, the Lancia Delta HF was the fastest 1600cc car around.

The rally version of the Delta was the Delta S4 which marked two significant milestones in Lancia's history: it was the first model to have four-wheel drive and a combined supercharging/turbocharging system was employed in the engine. The Delta S4 project got under way in April, 1983 under the leadership of Abarth engineers. Trials were started in June, 1984 and the new rally weapon of the Fiat Group quickly proved better than its predecessor, the Lancia Rally. The decision to use the Delta was taken partly to satisfy Lancia's image requirements and partly because its dimensions fitted the bill. As 200 had to be built for homologation purposes, a limited number were offered for sale. The Abarth-designed in-line 4 cylinder engine had a bore of 88.5mm and stroke of 71.5mm. The 1759cc unit could boast of at least 400bhp at 8000rpm.

It had a dream debut result of 1st and 2nd on the 1985 Lombard RAC Rally and only just failed to clinch the 1986 Rally Championship for Manufacturers.

The cockpit was totally different from anything found in a road-going Lancia.

THE STAKES ARE RAISED

The HF deserved to be a winner. For the enthusiast it was the best Delta ever to have left the Chivasso factory and was a genuine successor to the much loved Fulvia HF coupes. It was also, without doubt, one of the best performance saloons around and offered serious competition to models from the larger manufacturers.

Another turbo being launched in Italy at the same time as the Delta HF was the De Tomaso Innocenti. The car's three cylinder Daihatsu engine was fitted with an IHI turbocharger which increased the power from 52 to 76bhp and top speed to 100mph.

Another Italian car maker that was busy bringing out an important new model was Alfa Romeo. The Sud was not a name that the state-owned company wished to keep in their model line-up and the 33 that replaced the ageing car was totally different in its styling. Although they were approximately Sud size and shared the same floorpan and wheelbase, the skin was entirely new, developed way beyond the Sud concept to bring it into line with buyer requirements in the '80s, which was another way of saying performance, economy, mechanical refinement, space efficiency and aerodynamics. It was designed by Alfa Romeo themselves in conjunction with Guigiaro.

By following the trend to a modern notchback shape, they were trying to stretch across a broader spectrum of classes and prices so that by the time the Alfa-Nissan arrived later in the year, their range of cars would have fewer gaps than ever before. Thus the 33 shape recalled the lines of the Giulietta to try and win sales in that class while at the same time its hatchback utility would suit another market segment.

There were three versions at first: a 1.3 litre, a 1.5, and a top of the range Gold Cloverleaf loaded with the expected goodies of up-market cars. It was, however, the same mechanically as the run-of-the-mill 1.5. All were five-door models.

For Alfa Romeo, the 33 was obviously of vital importance. It was their first new model since the Alfa Six and was destined to be a cornerstone in the company's fight to regain a hold on the European market. It was by no means a sports car and it would need the introduction of the 33 Green Cloverleaf in mid-'84 to regain the attention of the enthusiast.

As already mentioned, Fiat's starting point for the attack on the hot hatchback market was the 105TC and the very hot Abarth 125TC, not introduced into Britain. After the facelift of the rather ugly range earlier in 1983 where the Stradas had lost some of the awful plastic addendums, decreased in weight, gained better aerodynamics and a lot more refinement - the 105TC and 125TC accordingly became much more desirable choices. An even hotter creation, however, was now waiting in the wings.

Despite having only 5bhp more than the 125TC, the 130TC re-asserted Fiat's determination to remain top of the hot hatch class in the normally aspirated class. Eschewing fuel injection, they chose a pair of twin-choke Weber 40DCOE carburettors which did the job well but were not up to the best of the injected cars. The carburettors were ably backed up by the Magneti Marelli Digiplex electronic ignition, a fully-mapped system that ensured cold starting, steady low-speed running and spark plug life.

The result was not so much that peak power was 130bhp at 5900rpm, but rather that the torque stayed above 110lb/ft all the way from 2000 to 6000rpm with 130lb/ft peak at 3500rpm, easily beating any rival. Together with the sturdy, close-ratio ZF gearbox and some drag-reducing tweaks on the body, such as the perspex window deflectors, the hot-shot motor reached a maximum top speed of 118mph and a standstill to 60mph of 8.3 secs. It was faster through the gears than any other car in the class and the acceleration did not even tail off when in fifth gear thanks to the close ratio gearing. It would rev smoothly all the way to the red line at 6250rpm. Gearchanging for town work, however, was too heavy.

With a fuel tank holding a fraction over 12 gallons, the fact that it only averaged 27mpg when touring and just under 24mpg when pressed hard and in town, still enabled it a range of over 300 miles.

For a car so swift, the kickback through the steering was pretty negligible, but it did snatch under heavy acceleration. Near the limit, the 130TC felt neutral when cornering, understeering initially then turning into oversteer, but not as gently as the Golf. In the wet, however, it was a different story as their was not enough grip from the front and the car had to be treated with respect to avoid understeering off the road. Lifting off in mid-corner in the dry, though, caused only a slight tightening of the line. Steering at parking speeds was rather heavy.

THE STAKES ARE RAISED

The fine handling was paid for with a rough ride. The firm suspension did not allow the car to be deflected in any way, but it did feel as though it wanted to enlarge each hole it entered, the shock of which transmitted itself to the driver. This made it rather a tiring car to drive compounded by the high cabin noise level.

It was an exciting car to drive, and was closer to being a competition car than either the Golf GTi, Astra GTE or Escort XR3i, but despite its many refinements, the 130TC was still no direct competitor to any of them. The 125TC had had a difficult role to play because it failed to match the civility of its major rivals and failed to offer any more performance. The 130TC came closer, but still did not equal, the oppositions' all-round efficiency - but it now had a fairly wide advantage over all of them in outright performance, and so had to be taken seriously. With an asking price similar to that of the Golf, the choice for the buyer between them all was one of purchasing either the Fiat, an out-an-out road burner with few compromises to comfort and economy or purchasing a civilised sports hatch that each scored higher points when it came to refinement and overall efficiency.

The Fiat Strada Abarth 130TC had a mean, aggressive look.

Its pronounced rear aerofoil, larger bore exhaust, lowered skirts and Abarth logo left you in no doubt about its performance potential.

Unlike most contenders in the hot hatchback race, Fiat still used carburettors in their projectiles.

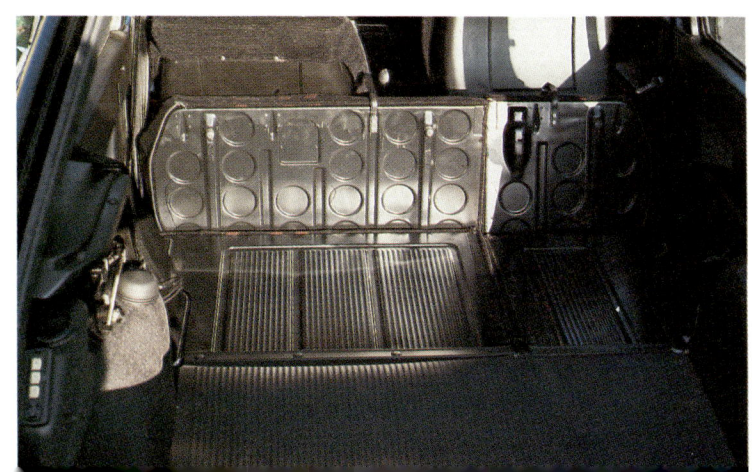

As a utility vehicle, the Fiat's rear seats folded away allowing a large, flat area for storage.

THE STAKES ARE RAISED

It was in the autumn of 1983 that Volkswagen made their nine year leap when they introduced the Golf II in Germany, coming to Britain the following February, followed by the GTi in May. During this time, six million VW Golfs had been produced a staggering half a million of which were the GTi's.

While losing the visual impact and crispness the old GTi had, the new look Golf was disappointingly similar to the outgoing model. Ital Design, who had penned the original design which was by now becoming to look just a little dated, were asked to submit ideas about the new model, but these were rejected in favour of VW's own in-house suggestions. 10 other proposals were considered before the go-ahead was given to the conservative approach which so closely shadowed the look of the previous model. It was true to form, however, for VW to follow this route seeing what they had done with the Scirocco, Polo, Passat in their second versions, the idea behind it being the wish to preserve continuity, customer loyalty and resale values.

Even though the new model kept to the spirit of the old, every panel was different as was the bumper and sloping grille and it also differed in weight and size - it was re-thought from the floorpan up. Its softer lines and 6.7in extra length gave it a better Cd figure of 0.34 compared to the old model's figure of around 0.40. It was remarkable how well VW scored on the aerodynamic front, given that their car did not use bodywork 'kinks' in strategic places, flush side-glass or even flush fitting door handles.

Apart from the leap forward in aerodynamic sophistication, it had improved luggage and cabin room, economy, performance, handling and ride, service ease, corrosion protection and just about every other relevant characteristic - to make it once again the best most progressive car in its class, but the body shape did not make the buyers aware of it.

Along comes the Mark II. The Mark II version of the Golf GTi looked less aggressive than the model it replaced, but more than before, was a wolf in sheep's clothing.

Inside the seats were comfortable and the gear lever had a golf ball atop it.

A five-door version of the GTi was introduced into Britain in January, 1985.

A combination of the increase in length, wheelbase (3in to 97.4in) and width (2.1in to 65.6in) which enlarged the rear passenger space and luggage area by 30% together with the improved ride turned the machine into a full, long distance runner. A rear axle location helped benefit the roadholding and the braking was improved. Its exterior dimensions were now similar to the Astra GTE's.

The beautifully smooth engine now had more torque which was 114lb/ft at 3100rpm while its 112bhp were delivered at 5500rpm instead of the previous 5800rpm. The Mark II was a marginally slower to 60mph than the older model, taking 8.6secs against 8.4secs, and was but 1mph faster, with a top speed of 114mph.

It was not increased performance that Volkswagen's engineers were looking for, but an increase in civility and refinement. This may not have been to the purists' delight, but by refining the ride, retaining its tremendous handling and passenger comfort and increasing the space, it once again became the car to beat in the hot hatchback stakes although with its increase in price of over £1000 from that of the last of the Mark I's, it was considerably more expensive than its rivals.

The Wolfsburg engineers were also working on a beefed-up version of the Polo which could long have been realised in GTi form if only the big 1.8 litre engine would have fitted under the compact car's bonnet. But since the capacity of the small 1.3 litre could not be increased much beyond its present stage, chief engine designer Peter Hofbauer resorted to a supercharger to boost the maximum power output from 75 to 118bhp. Unfortunately the combination of blower, intercooler and fuel injection system was considerably more expensive than a conventional turbocharger installation, which at that time was favoured by the VW's cost accountants. So no decision concerning a Polo GTi was made.

THE STAKES ARE RAISED

The 1.8 litre engine remained a delight, but the new body lacked the crispness of its predecessor.

The skinny spare wheel was only good for a maximum of 50mph.

From the rear, only the air dam and lettering gave away the GTi's identity.

THE STAKES ARE RAISED

The Ford Fiesta also underwent a facelift in the second half of 1983. The clever thing about Ford's, though, was that the Fiesta looked more like a new car and echoed the manufacturer's styling idiom with its rounded nose and flanks.

Apart from the alteration to the car's nose, it was the interior that received the most attention and received a neat dashboard, excellent seats and tasteful trim. It was also quieter.

The revised XR2 also received the engine the marketing men said it could not possibly have originally - the 1597cc engine, possible since the Escort had been uprated with injection status. The twin-choke Weber the XR2 utilised enabled the engine to produce 96bhp at 6000rpm and 97.4lb/ft of torque at 4000rpm giving a top speed of 110mph.

A nice balance was struck between ride and handling but it needed a determined hand to go fast

as the nervous feel of the car on the limit, which in fact was mis-information as it could remain glued to the road tenaciously, created a psychological barrier it was difficult to breach. It was very much a boy racer's car of the traditional kind and had the looks to match the performance.

1983 was the year when other manufacturers seriously began to threaten the dominance of the Golf GTi. Volkswagen responded twice, although the planning, particularly of the Mark II, pre-dated the decade. Ford's XR3i and General Motors' Astra/Kadett GTE were certainly as good as the Golf in many respects, and the Renault, with their Gordini Turbo, and the Fiat group, with the Lancia Delta HF and Abarth 130TC, were pushing the boundaries with regard to sheer performance. Unfortunately for the patriotic, the offerings based on the Metro were not up to par.

THE STAKES ARE RAISED

The new shape Fiesta XR2 was very appealing and was helped by Ford's attention to detail.

Now equipped with the 1.6 CVH engine, the XR2 could show a clean pair of heels to many a fancied larger engined rival.

It was in August, 1983 that the entire Fiesta range was announced in revised form. The most noticeable difference was the restyled front end, although the interior and rear had also been treated.

CHAPTER FOUR

THE GOING GETS TOUGH

It was in 1984 that the Japanese manufacturers began to make their presence felt in force. Making their entries were examples from Honda and Daihatsu while Mitsubishi had another stab with a revised Hatchback Turbo.

Early in the year, the all-new Civic range was introduced to Britain. There were three models altogether - the CRX, a three-door hatchback, similar in concept to the Polo and the Shuttle.

Making cars go fast is easy; it is building in the roadholding, handling and ride quality that are difficult. Difficult enough, in fact, for the Japanese makers to have botched it up every time until now.

In one concerted effort, Honda had Europanised their new Civics and made them outstandingly good, not just by Japanese standards, but by any yardstick. They achieved it by doing something that no one had ever thought of before, they shipped cars, engineers and suspensions from Japan and, using all the expertise and help they could get in Europe, sorted them out once and for all.

Thus, the CRX, for example, combined a lot of performance with firm, taut yet communicative ride that was accurately controlled and precisely damped.

Reinforcing their links with the Williams–Honda Grand Prix Racing team, a special one-off version of the Honda Civic CRX was 'Canonised' and presented as a prize to a lucky photographic competition winner.

The rear 'seat' was suitable only for children.

The Honda Civic CRX was a gem of a car. From one's first impression until one was behind the wheel, the car delights in every respect, and was one of the most exciting Hot Hatchbacks there was.

The CRX was the smallest and lightest in the Civic family, weighing in with a kerb weight of only 835kg. This compared with the 848kg of the Civic GT which was itself a light car for its class. Weight was saved with the use of Honda Polymer Alloy, a mixture of ABS plastic and polycarbonate on the areas of the car that were more susceptible to rust and knocks, namely on the lower side flanks and at the front below the bonnet line. It had a drag factor of .33cd which was unmatched by most of its competitors and was quite an achievement for a car of its short dimensions (144.7 in), only 2 inches longer in wheelbase than the Metro. It had a slippery shape, frameless windows, a flush-mounted windscreen, semi-concealed wipers, recessed door handles, 30°-inclined headlights and a smooth curved rear window. Its large rear spoiler and front air dam helped stability at high speed.

On the alloy wheels, which were fitted as standard, were 175/70HR13 tyres, the same as on the Civic GT. These provided good grip in all road conditions and gave the car a muscular, beefy look.

Underneath the bonnet was the same light alloy 74 × 86.5mm undersquare engine with its digital fuel injection which had first been seen on this model. The torque was the same as on the Civic GT, 96lb/ft torque at 4500rpm and produced 100bhp at 5750rpm. The unit was exactly the same as on the Civic GT including the 3 valves per cylinder, two inlet and one exhaust, crossflow head design and the chambers themselves were of the pent-roof design to increase efficiency. Siamesed bores were used in the cylinder block to save weight and decrease the length of the engine. In the interests of saving weight, the con rods were lightweight and the air cleaner was plastic. The distributor was attached to the end of the camshaft and the oil pump attached directly to the crankshaft, all in the name of simplicity. The transverse engine propelled the car through its front wheels.

The unconventional torsion bar and MacPherson strut front suspension was introduced on this model, doing away with the coil springs of previous Civics, and later made its way onto the Civic GT, allowing for the low bonnet line. At the rear there was a rigid beam axle located by trailing arms and a panhard rod replacing the independent MacPherson system seen on previous models. Steering was by rack and pinion. There were ventilated discs at the front and drums at the rear.

THE STAKES ARE RAISED

From all sides, the car was a stunner and could fly on the track or along winding roads. The engine (opposite) was the same unit as that found in the Civic GT, but it gave way to the 16-valve unit in 1986.

CHAPTER FOUR

The interior was markedly different from the Civic GT. The most noticeable aspect was the lack of a real back seat, there being something approaching a dug-out which folded down to present a flat deck with access via quite a high sill at the back. When the seat was in position, however, there was simply no head or leg room, and even for children, it was uncomfortable.

Maximum use was made of space in the interior and there was not any feeling of claustrophobia despite the car being quite small.

The dashboard was well laid out but the trim was of average quality - the tricot upholstery on the car slightly cheapened it. A digital clock broke up the expanse of dark plastic in front of the passenger and in the centre there was a dash-top box, as long as a cheque book and deep enough to place a notebook and a bunch of keys inside, which the author found to be one of the most convenient items in the car. A digital clock with stereo cassette facility came as standard.

There was an electric sun-roof which in the test car did not operate too well. Although a push of the switch opened the sun-roof, the runners were not greased enough, or the motor not strong enough, to open it fully, resulting in a draught coming straight onto the top of the head. When closing, there was not sufficient strength for the lid to be completely closed unless given a helping hand, which could be a little dangerous if carried out while driving along. As there was not sufficient room inside, the roof actually opened and slid back on top of the car which could not have done much for the aerodynamics.

Heating and ventilation were first class with six push-button controls. The position chosen was identified by an amber light which was dimmed during night-time driving. The heat and airflow could be varied from the huge number of vents and slots. One criticism, though, was that, like the Civic GT, it needed the boost to push the air into the cockpit as the ram air was not enough unless going at great speed.

As mentioned the level of trim was about average for a Japanese car, with perhaps too much plastic for European tastes. There was not even token carpet at the bottom of the doors. Good quality carpets, however, were fitted all round which undoubtedly helped reduce road noise.

Driving the car was a delight. It was in the tradition of the blue-blooded sports car manufacturers. Sitting in the driving seat, all the controls came nicely to hand, with the stalk on the left being the switch for the wipers, that on the right being the indicator switch as well as the light switch. The seats were comfortable but needed a little more lateral support to be completely satisfactory. The back positioning was slightly difficult to adjust to one's complete satisfaction. There was plenty of headroom for even the tallest driver in any of the seat's positions.

In front of you were the two large round dials housing the tachometer and the speedometer with the smaller water temperature gauge on the left and the fuel gauge on the right. They were free from reflection and at night were attractively illuminated. However the switches for the rear screen heater, the rear fog lamps and the sun roof were dotted about the dash and were not illuminated at night. There were a number of warning lights on the dash as well. A warning buzz was emitted if the lights were left on and the door was opened.

The start up was not instantaneous, with a few whirrings before the engine fired. The water temperature rose before that of the oil because of the instalment of an oil/water heat exchanger below the oil filter which also stabilised the coolants during high-speed motoring.

The gear slipped smoothly into first gear as it did in all gears except fifth which needed a more definite motion to engage. Pedal movement was also smooth. Over 4000rpm and the car really came on song and began to fly. At 6500rpm in 1st gear the CRX was travelling at 34mph, in 2nd gear 57mph, third gear 85mph and fourth and fifth gears at 117mph. 60mph was reached 8.8 secs just after changing into third. Mid range acceleration was par for the class with 30-50mph in fourth gear reached in 8.4 secs. 50-70mph in the same gear was completed in 9.1 secs. At this rate, fuel consumption obviously suffered, but an overall fuel consumption of 33.6mpg was fairly representative.

Reversing was a slight problem with the high rear wing and it took a little getting used to. A useful addition was the footrest for the driver's left foot. Various noises made themselves felt while driving the car. At rest, the engine ticking over, there was a perceptible buzz which came from the nearside rear, possibly from the fuel pump. Other odd rattles came from the rear, while the clutch operation emitted a low hiss which at first sounded more of a hi-fi noise until it became obvious that it was linked with the operation of the clutch. Noise level below 3000rpm was confined to tyre noise and the exhaust boom, but at engine speeds above 3000rpm and over 70mph, the noise became more of a roar of the wind, partly due to the seamless windscreen.

The steering on the car was good, going in the direction it was pointed, with little body roll. However it was happier on twisty roads than on motorways. At extreme speeds into corners, understeer could be induced, but it was predictable. Take your foot off the throttle in mid-corner, and the car tucked in sharply but still controllably. Handling was superb although the ride was a little on the choppy side, with the short suspension movements being mainly to blame. The brakes were progressive and nicely balanced, with a tendency to weave when used under extreme conditions being the only black mark.

Overall this was very much an enthusiast's car, being a two seater with the back seat useful for children only. It had the Honda name, probably the most charismatic of the Japanese motoring names, but at £6595 in the U.K., it was a little on the expensive side compared to some of its rivals.

The Japanese are masters at finding gaps among the conventional European small car classes and plugging them: the Daihatsu Charade did this very well. It dropped neatly between the Metro and Fiesta, smaller than a Polo, bigger than a Panda. And if size class is not enough, it came with a 1.0 litre three cylinder engine that saved on weight and friction, leading the fuel economy stakes.

A sporty turbo version was also included in the range, stretching the model up in performance terms to match the 1300s it competed with in many markets. It had a tiny IHI turbocharger blowing through an Aisan carburettor which boosted peak power from 51 to 68bhp and took the maximum speed in fifth gear to just over 100mph.

That kind of output in a small, lightweight (1622lb) car gave acceleration way above the one litre class, and was well-matched to cars like the naturally aspirated MG Metro.

The Mitsubishi Colt Hatchback Turbo made a fresh appearance in distinctive new clothes as an eye-catching three-door, top-of-the-range sportster that price-wise met head-on the best of the opposition.

The engine increased in size from 1400 to 1597cc and now delivered 123bhp at 5500rpm and a greater torque which peaked at 137lb/ft at 3000rpm but it performed no better than many of its rivals. Also the turbo lag was more than one expected from a company which by now had such experience with the technology.

The Mitsubishi Colt 1600 Turbo Hatchback.

THE GOING GETS TOUGH

From the rear, the air dam and the turbo logo in red lettering were the most prominent features.

The 4 cylinder OHC 1597cc engine produced 123.3bhp at 5500rpm giving the Colt 1600 Turbo a top speed in excess of 120mph.

Modern design technology allowed for the maximum use of space.

The engine revved freely all the way to the red line at 6000rpm which gave maximum speeds of 39, 56, 82 and 108mph in ther first four gears and top speed of 121mph in the long-striding fifth gear which made cruising at 100mph, 4500rpm very easy to take. This overdrive fifth gear helped with regard to economy, but returning an overall average of 25mpg, it was still much thirstier than any of its rivals.

With a weight distribution of 63 per cent front, 37 per cent rear, straight-line stability was good, but under hard acceleration, such was the feedback coming through the steering, that you had to hold onto the wheel hard as it fought to go its own way. At parking speeds, though, the steering was heavy.

Understeer was the major characteristic when piling into a corner, the tyres howling long before breakaway happened. Take your foot off the accelerator, and the nose immediately tucked in, needing correction at the steering wheel.

The ride, as can be expected, was firm, and although the car had excellent front seats, journeys could become tiring and uncomfortable over long distances. As with its predecessor, it could cope with the smoother surfaces, but once larger holes were hit, a harsh vertical movement occurred.

With a price tag of £7749 it more or less level pegged with the GTi, Fiat Strada Abarth and Lancia Delta Turbo. Other rivals like the Escort XR3i and Vauxhall Astra GTE were appreciably cheaper. The opposition to the blown Colt was thus formidable, but the Japanese car, despite its slightly uncouth character, held enough charm to tempt some customers away from the more commonly seen European models.

The 1987 styling change on the Colt 1600 Turbo Hatchback (below) included new front grille and bonnet, redesigned bumpers front and rear, wheel arches, repositioned side indicator lights and rear licence plate light with the overall length of the Turbo body reduced by 30mm.

THE GOING GETS TOUGH

It was the German cars that were the target of Peugeot's new model that was introduced at the 1984 Geneva Show. At this time, their 205 range had become extremely fashionable, saving the company from the gloom it seemed to be continually descending into. So popular was the little car that daily production was being stepped up to a target of between 1600-1800 units a day, exceeding its own record of 1350 cars a day achieved with the 504 in 1978. Peugeot's other popular model from the past, the 204, had first place in the sales charts for three successive years in 1969, 1970 and 1971, but because it was little known outside France, daily production never exceeded 925 units. The twin arrival of the GTi and the image-boosting rally 16 Turbo would help even further with sales.

No matter what the condition, the exciting Peugeot 205T16 was a winner, winning the Manufacturer's rallying title in 1985 and 1986.

A road-going version of the 205 Turbo 16 was built at Poissy over a three month period in late 1984, just 27 months after the first design work was started. 200 examples were made, all left-hand drive, for homologation purposes.

THE GOING GETS TOUGH

The 205 Turbo 16 was built in three sections. They included a monocoque main body shell in pressed steel, a front section, also in steel, with cross members, panel and box sections, and a steel tubular rear section, including a chassis for mounting the engine and drive components. To this were attached the main body panels, which were made from either sheet steel or polyester. The power unit was a development of the XU series fitted to the 205GTi, but in the Turbo 16, it had a capacity of 1775cc. It was a four cylinder, in-line unit with four valves per cylinder and twin overhead camshafts. At the start of its life, it developed 200bhp at 6750rpm and a maximum torque of 255lb/ft at 4000rpm.

With their first entry in the hot hatchback category, Peugeot got it right. The car not only looked good, but it was wonderful in pretty well every department. The handling was excellent, the ride good, engine smooth, brakes effective and it was extremely rapid. It also put Peugeot back in the top echelon of car makers.

The big question it had to answer was how would it fare against the Golf II. First company estimations reckoned on making 80 a day, but as it turned out, the Parisian company greatly underestimated its demand as the car took the world by storm and even when they were producing 200 a day in the autumn, they still could not meet European demand!

The heart of the car was the 1580cc transverse engine which shared a similar specification to that of the 305GT, but as it was now fitted with Bosch L-Jetronic fuel injection and a 10.2:1 compression ratio, the power output was raised to 105bhp at 6250rpm and 99lb/ft of torque at a high 4000rpm, but which remained flexible due to the high gearing. It was willing to rev smoothly all the way up to the ignition cut-out at 6250rpm.

To cope with the extra power, there were a number of suspension changes to the car. The front spring rates were trebled compared to the 205GR and the rest of the dampers and springs were also stiffened. The anti-roll bars were altered as well, being reduced in thickness on the front and increased at the back.

The good power-to-weight ratio enabled acceleration from rest to 60mph in 8.7 secs, 100mph in under 30 secs, and a top speed of 117mph. As impressive was the pulling power between 30-70mph in upper gears, thanks in part to the low gearing.

The 11 gallon tank allowed a range little short of 400 miles if driving was restrained, otherwise a return of about 31mpg would be seen.

In overall handling, balance and roadholding the GTi was phenomenal and set new front-wheel drive standards. The car was fairly neutral with a trace of understeer in the fast bends but responded instantly to even a flick of the wrists and would change direction at ridiculous speeds. On the absolute limit its manners were impeccable - the tail would come round gently, and it would oversteer gently if you backed off in a corner. The price paid for this, though, was an uncompromisingly hard suspension resulting in a "stiffish" ride and at low speeds in tight bends there tended to be a great kickback through the wheel. Altogether, though, the overall balance of the car was outstanding.

In one go, Peugeot had produced the best sporting hatchback, and if available two years before, may well have stolen the crown from the 1600cc Golf GTi. Making a break from the familiar shape, its cheeky, rounded lines were an instant eye-catcher and coupled with its performance and chuckability was destined to do its bit in further reviving the fortunes of Peugeot.

The fabulous Peugeot 205GTi.

THE GOING GETS TOUGH

The Peugeot's good looks and a shape that stood it apart from the super-mini crowd all contributed to the success of the 205GTi.

Luggage space in the 205 was more than adequate with the rear seat folded down.

The heart of the car was the 1580cc transverse engine which shared a similar specification to that of the 305GT. Access to it was also very good.

THE GOING GETS TOUGH

Not just conceived, but born a full decade before Peugeot's new rascal came bursting in on the scene, the Renault 5 had been number one in France for an extraordinary 12 years and had produced 5.5 million units. Even in 1980, it reached a new record level of sales and took 16 per cent of the French market. Its replacement, though, had caused many a headache to the Regie's planners who were worried by the prospects especially as Renault was in the midst of a massive financial crisis. Like Volkswagen with the Golf they decided to stick to the R5 name and give it to a different model. During the last months of life of the old R5, the model became the Laureate in an effort to avoid confusion between the coming model and the departing one.

After spending £400 million on a ground up re-vamp, the Super Five, as it was unofficially christened, looked much the same as the old car. It was actually 2.36in longer and wider, but the shapes were so similar that it took more than a moment to notice the many detail changes. It was also 10 per cent lighter, 6 per cent more aerodynamically efficient and had 20 per cent more glass.

Mechanically, the Renault was completely transformed and now fell into line with the rest of the supermini class. The old back-to-front, north-south gearbox and engine layout, which needed a complicated linkage, was replaced by a conventional transverse engine and transmission.

At the time of its introduction in the autumn of 1984 in France and in the spring of 1985 in Britain, there was not a performance version offered. The Renault 5 GT Turbo was due to replace the Gordini Turbo but would not appear on the British market until mid-summer, so meanwhile the Peugeot 205 bandwagon rolled on.

Similar to the model it replaced, the new Renault 5 shape remained timeless.

Renault, though, by now established as Europe's major turbo-car manufacturer, had introduced the 11 Turbo into Britain in April, but where it differed from the Regie's other offerings was that it used the smaller, lighter Garrett AiResearch T2 turbocharger, not the T3. While the engine response was better, there was a sacrifice in ultimate power so while it used the same 1397cc pushrod overhead valve engine as the 5 Gordini Turbo, the end product was by no means the same.

A maximum 105bhp was delivered at 5500rpm instead of the 110bhp at 6000rpm of the R5 Gordini Turbo but much more impressive was the low-down 2500rpm point where maximum torque was up from 108lb/ft to 119lb/ft, with 90 per cent of that figure available between 2000 and 5000 revs. This massive torque power put punch in each gear enabled the R11 Turbo to accelerate rapidly, reaching 60mph from standstill in 8.5 secs and 90mph in under 20 secs. Only in the fourth gear maximum did the pace slacken.

With the ignition-cutting rev limiter cutting-in at 6200rpm, the maxima speeds in each gear were 32, 54, 76 and 103mph with a top speed of 116mph.

The 11 Turbo was successfully given the usual sports model treatment with regard to suspension and steering. While acknowledging that this was a rapid model, Renault did not want to provide it with fine handling at the expense of a harsh ride, and yet it was both safe and grippy in that department with only a trace of understeer. Even in the wet it gripped the road well and showed good balance. What let it down was the poor seating inside. Although the front seats gave good lateral support, they lacked lumbar support and were very uncomfortable after a while. The driving position was not particularly praiseworthy either, the pedals being rather too close together and the leather-trimmed steering wheel set too high. In the back, too, the seat space was poor and short of leg and knee room.

Apart from these fairly minor quibbles, the smart Renault 11 Turbo was an easy car to live with combining performance with civility as well as having a high standard of equipment.

Up until this time, in 1984, Ford had managed to steer clear of the burgeoning turbocharging bandwagon, choosing other paths to high performance.

Enter the Escort RS Turbo in February, 1985, a homologation special, just like its predecessor, the RS1600i, with an initial production run of just 5000 to obtain Group A homologation so as to be able to compete more competitively in international races and rallies. Ford's first production venture into turbocharging was rather cautious, involving a lightly modified CVH engine and a body re-style of the popular XR3i adding colour-matched flared arches, tail spoiler, Orion-type grille and attractive seven spoke 15in alloy wheels.

THE GOING GETS TOUGH

The addition of attractive side skirts, sills and spoilers gave the Ford Escort Turbo RS great looks to match its supercar performance.

THE GOING GETS TOUGH

To get over the problem of torque reaction affecting the steering, Ford broke new ground in one area with the RS Turbo and that was it was the first front-wheel drive car to use a Ferguson viscous coupling, a type of limited-slip differential, to help improve handling, traction and tyre life.

Ford's Special Vehicle Engineering Department, under Rod Mansfield, was given 12 months to produce the RS, and they achieved a remarkable result: a car that was head-and-shoulders above any previous Escort: faster, more refined and smoother, and a car which not only had substantially better handling, but also an overall ride quality which was better. It also lacked too much engine noise, was less prone to booms at high revs and the Ferguson viscous coupling stopped any excessive wheelspin when powering out of a corner.

The engine was basically the 1596cc XR3i unit but modified to accept the turbo. It developed 130bhp at 6000rpm with 133lb/ft of torque at 3000rpm. Unhampered by turbo lag, acceleration was blood-stirring, reaching 60mph from standstill in 7.9 secs. The compression ratio was reduced to 8.3:1 from 9.5:1 with the use of heavy duty flat-topped pistons. Garrett provided the AiResearch T3 turbocharger which was limited to give a modest 7psi boost. The T2 was investigated, which would have given better low-down boost, but was turned down in favour of the T3 as it was necessary to have high boost pressures for competition work. An air/air intercooler was fitted, and the turbo forced air at 1.5 bar into the air intake of a new electronically controlled Bosch KE-jetronic injection system.

Boost began at around 2000rpm and was working hard by 2500rpm. Even in fifth gear, the Turbo was able to outperform a normal XR3i in the 30-50mph bracket and was superior to the Delta HF in this respect.

Fuel consumption suffered and dropped to an average of 26.5mpg and was certainly more thirsty than the XR3i, Golf GTi and Delta HF. At a cruising consumption of 29.0mpg its 10.6 gallon tank gave it a range of just about 300 miles.

On the road, it rode firmly on smooth roads, but was a little jarring over bumps but was controlled well enough so as not to be too bad. In handling, the car flattered and helped the driver. Take the corners at excessive speed and there was no trace of wheelspin, thanks to the viscous coupling which, by transferring some of the driving torque to the inside wheel, caused the car to be pulled into the bend. Progress therefore remained rapid.

Ford's off-the-shelf homologation special was well packaged for a car in this class. Its biggest asset was the engine which was smooth-running and flexible complemented by the outstanding grip, handling and ride. Its one big drawback was the price, which at £9250, was hard to justify when the Golf GTi was £7699 and the Lancia Delta HF £7990.

After the early Alfa Romeo 33s had been knocked for their lack of go, the 33 Green Cloverleaf was introduced in 1984, coming to Britain in June, and it looked good with its subtle exterior changes, such as alloy wheels with low profile tyres, new grille, body-colour bumpers, black door frames, sill extensions and front and rear spoilers, over the standard 33. Its engine was the familiar flat-four unit from the Alfasud - a short stroke (84x67.2mm) 1490cc boxer unit with a single cam for each bank of two cylinders fed by their own twin-choke Dellorto carburettor. The result was an impressive 24 per cent increase in power over the earlier Gold Cloverleaf with 105bhp at 6000revs and peak torque of 98.3lb/ft at a fairly high 4000rpm.

The ratios were closely spaced and low geared resulting in a 0-60mph time of 9.7 secs, although the free-revving engine and slick gearchange gave the impression of a good performance. With maximum speeds of 50mph in second, 70mph in third and 94mph in fourth, it was fifth gear that pulled the 33 the rest of the way to its 115mph maximum.

As the chassis was Alfasud in origin, the 33 was a lot of fun to drive, although other models had by this time surpassed that car's standards. Installed with the 105bhp engine, some deficiencies also showed up.

The steering was precise, but less so, and the engine was noisy. The handling was not up to the standard of the Sud and the ride was harsher in an effort to eradicate the torque steer.

While the driving position was uncomfortable even though the seats provided good lateral support, the rest of the interior was acceptable. It had rather a gloomy black cabin but in which there was generous accommodation space for both passengers and luggage. The sill of the hatchback, though, was unfortunately rather high and the seats did not fold flat. The steering wheel was adjustable on a vertical plane and took the instrument binnacle with it, although you could not lower it too far because of your knees.

Where the car scored over most of its rivals was in having five doors instead of three, but against that, it gave the impression of being a pretty and new body fitted onto tired old legs, and so consequently lacked the Alfa magic.

THE GOING GETS TOUGH

The Alfa Romeo Green Cloverleaf is the symbol of the company's specialist sports car. The 33 Green Cloverleaf had a more powerful engine than any other model in the range, but still lacked the punch of some of its rivals. It scored, though, by having a very pretty body which was further enhanced by the addition of large sill mouldings and light alloy wheels.

1984 was notable for the advent of the Peugeot 205GTi, a landmark for Peugeot and hot hatchbacks. Where it was becoming recognised that the hot hatchback market was beginning to stretch upwards to the junior executive level of car while still maintaining a presence in the 'super-mini' class, the distance between both extremes had gone so far as to be itself split into segments.

Thus, the Peugeot was not directly comparable to the new 1.8 Golf, for although both had three doors and only 200cc difference between them, they represented and dominated their respective segments.

The Golf was having a tougher time of it, what with the turbocharged offerings from Ford, Lancia and Colt, but still the car represented the best all round contender although there were many who did not like its softer new looks.

1985 promised even more models, some being revamps, and some freshly new, that would keep the German and French engineers in Wolfsburg and Paris busy developing their cars and not resting on their laurels.

CHAPTER FIVE

VARIATIONS ON A THEME

It was in late 1984 that Austin Rover announced the 2.0 MG Maestro EFi. In its original 1600 form, the car did not live up to expectations on the road and was more of a family car. The trouble was that Austin Rover were too eager to get a performance version of the car out and that did more harm than good. The twin-carb S-series engine was initially flawed by induction troubles that gave tricky hot starting and poor fuel consumption. Many of the 15,000 MG 1600 buyers must have been disappointed for not waiting for the stop-gap 1600 to run its course before being displaced by the O-series Lucas-injected 2 litre.

Compared with the superceded 1600, power was up by 12bhp from 103bhp at 6000rpm to 115bhp at 5500rpm. The increase in torque was even more telling - up from 100lb/ft at 4000rpm to a new high of 134lb/ft at only 2800rpm. The 2 litre had a good performance with a 0-60mph of 8.7 secs and a maximum top speed of 115mph, but it was the low and mid-range punch that was most impressive. It pulled from below 3000rpm with no fuss but at higher revs was a little thrashy, as were all O-series engines.

The Honda gearbox replaced the Volkswagen and was generally a smoother unit, but still had the tendency to baulk. Maximum speeds in each gear were 34mph in first, 58mph in second, 82mph in third and 107mph in fourth.

Fuel consumption was down on the 1600's, but still stood comparison with class rivals. Returning an average of 27.6mpg and a cruising figure of 34.7mpg, it meant that the 11 gallon fuel tank gave the car a range of almost 400 miles.

Compared to the flowing lines of the 5-door Alfa 33 Green Cloverleaf, those of the MG Maestro were disappointingly bland which not even the addition of spoilers or alloy wheels could disguise.

VARIATIONS ON A THEME

VARIATIONS ON A THEME

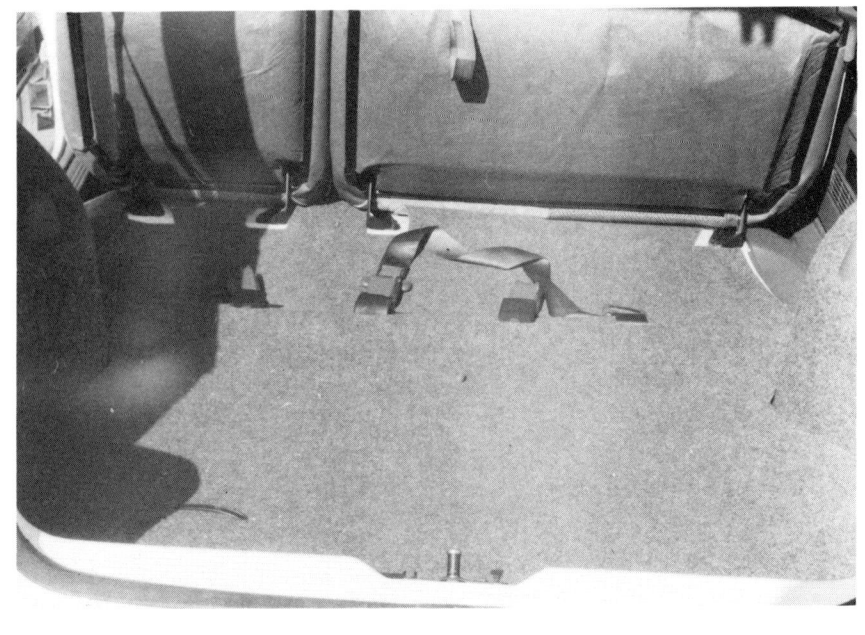

The interior spaciousness of the Maestro was the car's biggest asset. The interior decor was tastefully done as well. The driving position was good and all-round visibility excellent. The dials were easy to read but the dashboard itself was a little cluttered.

VARIATIONS ON A THEME

The Maestro offered plenty of leg-room and head-space was ample. At the back, the low sill allowed easy loading.

The Maestro's engine was an old unit, but the Lucas fuel injection gave it excellent performance. The acceleration was urgent and it gave out a good hearty growl.

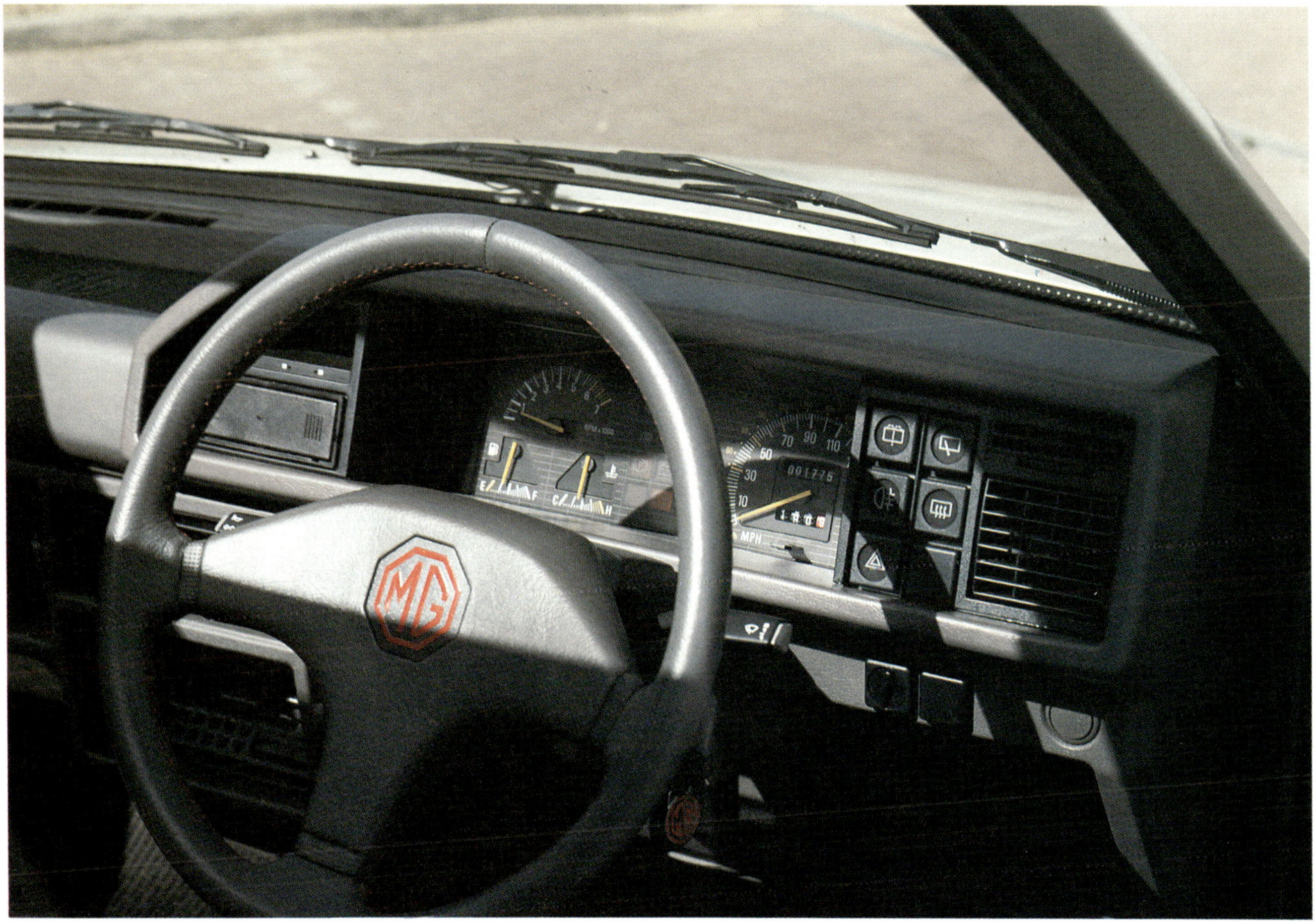

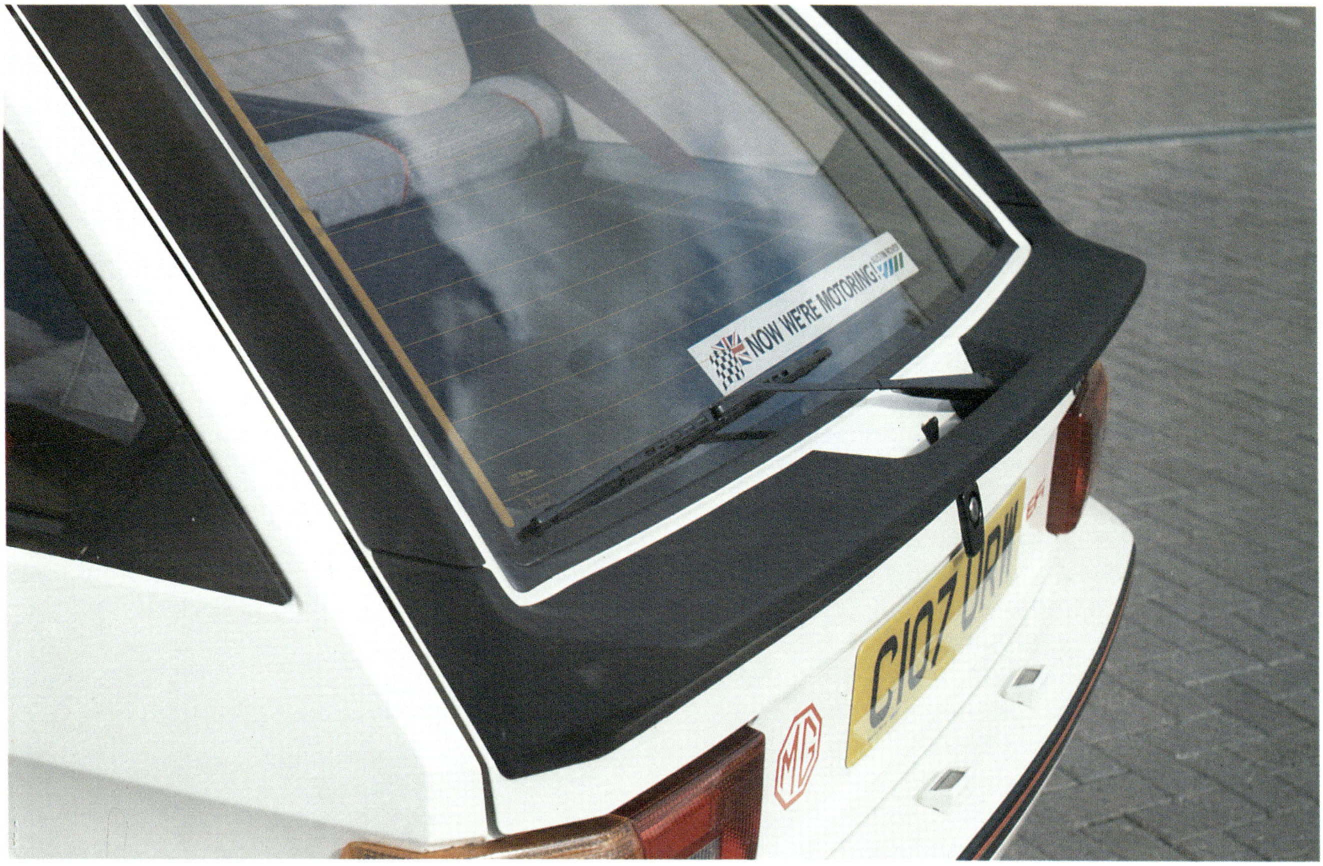
NOW WE'RE MOTORING!
C107 URW

VARIATIONS ON A THEME

There were few chassis and suspension modifications from the 1600, but the car was now tyred by low profile 175/65HR14's. However there was no adverse effect on the ride which remained impressive. The handling was also good. Torque steer had been eradicated and the car gripped the road well.

Full use was made of the five doors and interior space was excellent. The driving position was comfortable and the visibility marvellous. The dashboard, however, was disappointing but was the only minor point in an otherwise well thought out machine.

The MG was over £700 less than the Golf GTi, and although its performance was a little disappointing for a 2 litre with fuel injection, it nevertheless had a good mid-range punch. Its refinement over the older model was far better but it had yet to equal that of the Golf.

Shown at the 1984 Motor Show Austin Rover brought out a face lifted MG Metro Turbo where the front and interior were restyled and improved enormously, but it still needed a decent engine to complement its fine features. A unit that was 30 years old was not up to the job of competing with rivals who were featuring state of the art technology.

Also introduced in October 1984 was the revised Vauxhall Astra GTE. The original model had been as good as the original Golf GTi, but now the GTE itself was given a change of clothes. It was a controversial tear-drop shape that made it stand out dramatically from the other cars in its class, its streamlined body and aerodynamic aids now giving it a class best Cd value of 0.30. Against that, though, had to be offset the loss of headroom and poor visibility through the rear and side windows.

To make up for that, though, the car performed well, and was about the best mile-eating car of its class with over 120mph on tap. But its 0-60mph time of 9.1 secs was disappointing for a 115bhp hot hatch and its mid-range power delivery surprisingly weak. It was ultimately fast, though, and set new standards for a car of its power output, attaining a top speed of at least 120mph.

There were few mechanical changes from the superseded model, but the ratios were changed which allowed maximum speeds in the gears of 32mph in first, 50mph in second, 74mph in third and 97mph in fourth. Inside, the car received a digital dashboard layout, which was not of universal liking.

There was nothing unruly about the GTE's handling and showed almost neutral characteristics until driven hard when a trace of understeer crept in, yet it

VARIATIONS ON A THEME

In October, 1984 the Astra Mark II was announced with its aerodynamically efficient body, but remaining mechanically as before.

Already very quick, the GTE became even hotter after it had been through the hands of Irmscher, a West German company, with a distributor in England, that offered a range of sporty styling and performance equipment. Turbo Technics of Northampton turbocharged the engine using the Garrett T3 turbo and found an additional 35bhp which allowed the car to do a genuine 130mph, while acceleration from 0–60mph dropped by some 2 seconds to 7.3 seconds.

VARIATIONS ON A THEME

was ultimately not terribly rewarding to drive hard. As with the old GTE, its steering was low geared with 4.2 turns from lock to lock, but was a little too light. The car was well damped at speed, but could be quite harsh over bumpy surfaces.

Although the new GTE had a more efficient shape and was faster than the model it replaced, it fell short of the Golf by some margin. It was not that the new Vauxhall had any particular faults, but it was somehow disappointing in that it was not as exhilarating to drive as it looked on paper. Priced some £650 under that of the Golf it still had a lot of appeal, but being £300 more than the XR3i, it had its work cut out.

Another car that looked promising on its debut, in March 1985, was the Nissan Cherry Turbo ZX. Although it could reach a speed of 116mph and 0-60mph in a good 8.0 secs, the 114bhp 1.5 litre car could never be called refined. Its engine was rough and the transmission juddered badly when the turbo came in with a punch in the lower gears. The poorly chosen gear ratios did not help either. On the other hand, the Cherry had good steering and brakes and handled quite well, but at the expense of ride comfort. It was not a bad effort and what it offered was typical of Nissan with its strong emphasis on economy and reliability.

It was in August, 1983 that Nissan offered the Alfasud engined Cherry Europe and Europe GTi, followed two months later by the GTi Turbo, a Nissan-engined car. This lasted for 17 months before it underwent a facelift. In addition to changes to the interior, a deep front spoiler was added which helped high speed stability while the black lower panels and wheel arches gave the car a more purposeful air.

Arch rival Toyota also announced their contender for the hot hatchback market. It had only been a matter of when, not if, Toyota would bring out their example for they had all the ingredients scattered over different models, and it was just a question of assembling them all into one shell.

In the new generation Corollas, they had a front-wheel drive hatchback body, and in the Corolla Coupe GT had a 16-valve, twin-cam 1.6 engine that was potent enough for the job. When this was dropped into the front-wheel drive hatchback body, the result was a strong contender.

The work that went into Toyota's first hot hatchback was more than it might look on paper for it was immediately right, the company taking advantage of being late on the scene by learning every lesson from its already established rivals. It was helped by having a gem of an engine that was smooth and powerful and which also powered the MR2.

The unit developed 119bhp at 6600rpm and 103lb/ft of torque at 5000rpm. This produced an astonishing 0-60mph time of only 7.7 secs and a top speed 118mph. Its mid-range pulling power was top of the class but faster than 100mph, and the acceleration began to tail off.

Helped by a quick gearchange, such rapid acceleration was also provided by its rather short gearing which enabled top speeds in the first four gears of 34, 56, 81 and 110mph at the 7600rpm red line. With all this power on tap, economy suffered and a lowish

VARIATIONS ON A THEME

Toyota's first hot hatchback was the Corolla twin-cam and it was an immediate worthy challenger to the European models.

The shape of the Honda Civic was a revelation when it was first seen at the Frankfurt Motor Show in 1983. The wedge shape created by its low nose and kicked rear quarter made the car utterly different from any other hatchback on the road. Although the luggage area was fairly tight, the rear seat leg-room was good.

VARIATIONS ON A THEME

average of 27.7mpg was the result. Its tank capacity of 11 gallons, however, gave it a useful 400 mile range.

Handling and roadholding were exhilirating, but the steering was heavy even though a 10 per cent variable rack had been fitted to stop this. On dry roads, the grip was every bit as good as the Peugeot 205GTi's and did not deviate from the line when encountering bumps. Surprisingly ride comfort was not sacrificed to this end although it was naturally a little firm.

Inside the standards were still kept up. The steering position could not be criticised as there were a huge number of adjustments that could be made to the seat, although it might take a little time finding the ideal setting. Good lateral and lumbar support was provided which allowed long journeys being undertaken without becoming too tiring. The rest of the interior was spacious and well appointed.

In one bound, Toyota had presented a car that ranked alongside both the Peugeot 205GTi and Volkswagen GTi as a package offering overall speed and performance with tremendous gearchange, refinement, fabulous roadholding and good ride, in a spacious body. The largest Japanese car maker had now arrived, was there any stopping them?

The impressive Toyota Corolla GT was better than most of its European rivals in almost every aspect and was priced very competitively.

As if to rub salt into the wound, Honda came along with their answer in the junior hot hatchback class. The wondrous little coupe, the Civic CRX, was already a pacemaker in the sports car/hatchback category and ran the Peugeot 205GTi a close second on everything but interior space and comfort. Now, as if to answer criticism of lack of space in the CRX, Honda came up with a four-seater version, the Civic GT which replaced the short-lived Civic S.

Honda's answer to the hatchback styling theme was refreshingly different and yet aerodynamically efficient with a Cd factor of 0.35. Without the go-faster bits, such as extended wheel arches, aerofoils and spoilers, it did not look the part of a hot hatch, but it was, its understated body housing the same all-aluminium 1488cc engine that powered the CRX.

The 12-valve unit with the same contactless ignition and PGM-F1 electronic fuel injection and low compression ratio of 8.7:1 developed 99bhp at 5750rpm and 96lb/ft of torque at 4500rpm. With a gearchange that was every bit as good as that on the Toyota, the car accelerated from standstill to 60mph in 8.9mph and reached a top speed of 112mph. Its mid-range pulling power was every bit as good as its super-mini rivals with the exception of the Peugeot.

The extended air dam skirt on the Honda Civic GT was one of the subtle changes of appearance from that of others in the range. Other alterations included re-designed wheel covers and side protection moulding.

VARIATIONS ON A THEME

VARIATIONS ON A THEME

With the rear seat folded down, there was a great deal more luggage space available in the Honda Civic. The GT version was capable of a top speed of 112mph.

The 12-valve engine with the same contactless ignition and PGM-FI electronic fuel injection and low compression ratio of 8.7:1 as the CRX developed 99bhp at 5750rpm and 96lb/ft of torque at 4500rpm.

Top speeds were 34mph in second, 57mph in third and 85mph in fourth. Fuel economy was comparable to the little Peugeot averaging 31.1mpg overall and 38.5 at touring speeds. This gave the car a range of just under 400 miles with its 9.9 gallon fuel tank capacity.

The ride was hard but the car handled well at all times and in fact excelled the CRX. At the limit, the GT would begin to understeer in corners and the inside front wheel spin, but it was still fairly safe. Steering was light and precise.

Where the car fell down was inside. The instruments were about the best around, being legible and well planned, but what the car lacked was space. Lack of room for the luggage, rear passenger space was cramped, tiny boot space with a high sill and lack of headroom. To cap it all, the seats were thin and unsupportive.

It was priced at £6595, just below the asking price of £6645 for the Peugeot 205GTi and above the XR2's £6193 and Metro Turbo's £6371, but with only a few hundred pounds either way, the price differential was not going to be the determining factor. The Civic GT was an interesting alternative as

VARIATIONS ON A THEME

its shape was refreshingly different, and it offered good handling with quite an amount of power and good economy.

The continental manufacturers were now beginning to direct more and more of their models into the battle. In April, 1985, Citroen announced the BX Sport, a 121mph special of which only 2500 units would be made to test public reaction. However, such was the reception that it was elevated to a full production run for Europe, although the difficulty of routing the new exhaust manifold around the steering column for right-hand drive car precluded the possibility of it coming to Britain.

For its 1905cc capacity the Sport had a power output of 126bhp at 5800rpm and 124lb/ft of torque at 4200rpm. Instead of having fuel injection like most of its rivals, each cylinder was provided with an individual carburettor choke. It was a pity that a car as interesting as the BX Sport was not brought into the UK as it would have made a welcome addition. It was more akin, though, to the MG Montego and Ford Sierra XR4i because although it was a hatchback, its characteristics were more akin to a sporting saloon.

The BX Sport was a special version announced by Citroen in April, 1985. It was produced only in small numbers and was available only in left-hand drive. It outwardly differed in detail from the standard BX (shown) but was a great deal quicker.

Despite the good Delta range, topped by the fiery HF, Lancia were a car maker that were still in trouble in Britain in 1985. Seven years earlier they had sold 11,764 Lancias in the UK, in 1982 registrations were down to 5,170, the following year the figure was down to 3,461 and in 1984 the nadir was reached at 2,639. So it was with some expectation that the importers, Lancar, looked to the new model, the Y10, which went on sale in June, 1985.

There were three models, the Y10 Fire, Y10 Touring and Y10 Turbo. Designed by Lancia in close collaboration with Fiat and built at Fiat's Mirafiori works, it was smaller than a Metro yet aerodynamically more efficient than anything in its class and had an impressivley low Cd figure of 0.31 for such a short car. Its wedge nose, high roofline, flush sides and vertical tail all helped it in this respect.

Where the Y10 Fire model used the brand new Fire engine, the turbocharged version utilised the Brazilian made 1049cc unit. Fed by a twin-choke Weber 32 TLF/250 carburettor and Marelli Digiplex ignition system married to a Japanese IHI turbocharger, it delivered 85bhp at at 5750rpm and 90lb/ft at

Lancia's trend-setting Y10 range started with the FIRE, which derived its name from the Fully Integrated Robotised Engine. The engine cost £240 million to bring to fruition and was light, durable and needed little maintenance. The Y10 was a fraction over 133 inches long (2 inches shorter than a Metro, 10 inches less than a Fiesta) yet capable of transporting four adults in comfort.

VARIATIONS ON A THEME

2750rpm. Performance from the little unit was impressive and the car covered the 0-60mph time in 9.5 secs and reached a top speed of 112mph.

Where it came into its own was in urban driving, its nimble acceleration and small size ideal for the cut and thrust of conditions there. Where it was not so good was on the open road where the engine tended to roar rather harshly at anything over 5000rpm. And it was out of town that the poor ride comfort became more noticeable, long journeys becoming very tiring. Where it made up for it was in the handling, and the car could hurtle around country lanes and roundabouts at an astonishing rate with little understeer.

Fuel economy was an overall average of only 27mpg, which was quite some considerable amount less than comparable small cars. The touring figure of 37mpg was a little better.

This small hot hatchback enabled Lancia to have a foot in both the small and larger segments of the market, but unlike its bigger brother, the Y10 Turbo failed in its quest. Where the Delta HF Turbo was a very rapid tourer, capable of cross country and autostrada journeys in comfort, it seemed that the wrong emphasis had been given to the smaller model. It was well placed to be a fast, chic urban machine, but by compromising the ride in favour of handling, Lancia appeared to have chosen the wrong route to make it the best townie around.

A month later, Fiat, this time in their own name, had another try in the small turbocharged hatchback market, and this time they got a bullseye.

The Y10 Turbo was a good combination of power and refinement. The 1049cc overhead camshaft engine with turbo charger and intercooler produced 85bhp at 5750rpm. Adding the sporting touch to the exterior design was a front air dam, which incorporated additional lamp units, and a headlamp wash/wipe system.

The Fiat Uno Turbo was launched in Britain in July, 1985. The Uno's familiar three-door bodyshell was restrained with only slight styling changes, in particular, a new tailgate incorporating a spoiler and new protective bumpers incorporating in the front an air dam and fog lights.

To look at, there were few changes made to the standard Uno 70 body when the Japanese IHI turbocharger was dropped into it. There were the go-faster appendages, such as front air dam, which incorporated fog lights, spoiler on the hatch and alloy wheels which carried Pirelli P6s.

Underneath the bonnet, though, and the changes soon became apparent. The 1300cc was a purpose-built unit designed to take a turbo and incorporated all the latest technology. The block now had water-cooled linings, the all-alloy head with belt driven camshaft was new and the engine featured electronic ignition with a knock sensor and Bosch LE-Jetronic fuel injection. The turbocharger was supplemented by an inter-cooler and oil cooler.

The result was 105bhp at 5750rpm with 108lb/ft of torque at 3200rpm. The extra power meant a Strada/Ritmo gearbox in place of the usual Uno offering, along with a bigger clutch and equal length drive shafts. The result of all this was a car that was quicker by quite an amount than its rorty and macho 2 litre cousin, the Abarth 130TC. That it could achieve 124mph was simply outstanding from such a little unit, and the 0-60mph figure of 8.3 secs was also very spritely. When driven hard, the fuel consumption figures suffered, a figure of 26mpg

VARIATIONS ON A THEME

VARIATIONS ON A THEME

being normal, but at touring speeds, 34mpg was possible. With the 11 gallon tank, this gave the car a range of approximately 300 miles.

The engine was very free revving and went happily all the way to the 6400rpm red line. There was not any apparent lag and the delivery of its power was smooth and immediate.

Being slightly undergeared, the car accelerated well and recorded 27mph in first, 49mph in second, 75mph in third and 106mph in fourth. Not only was the mid range punch strong, but it also was there even at higher speeds.

There were very few changes to the chassis which unfortunately was not up to the same very high standard. The steering had been sharpened with a different rack, and gas-filled dampers and an anti-roll bar were added to the front, but ride was very hard. Understeer was the basic characteristic but the car remained stable when cornering even when the power was taken off half way round. Brakes were discs all round, ventilated at the front, and very effective.

It was a car that was tremendous fun to drive and at £6889 represented incredible value. It firmly belonged to the second breed of hot hatchback, the model that had been specially prepared for performance purposes rather than a hatchback that had been hotted up.

The Uno Turbo differed from the standard versions in the following respects: new, larger diameter exhaust pipe, a new intermediate silencer and chrome-plated silencer tailpipe; larger fuel tank; high pressure electric fuel pump mounted outside the tank; larger outboard constant velocity joints; larger diameter front wheel bearings; new $5\frac{1}{2}J \times 13$ aluminium alloy wheels; 17/60HR13 low profile tyres; it was thus able to cope with the extra power of the turbocharged engine.

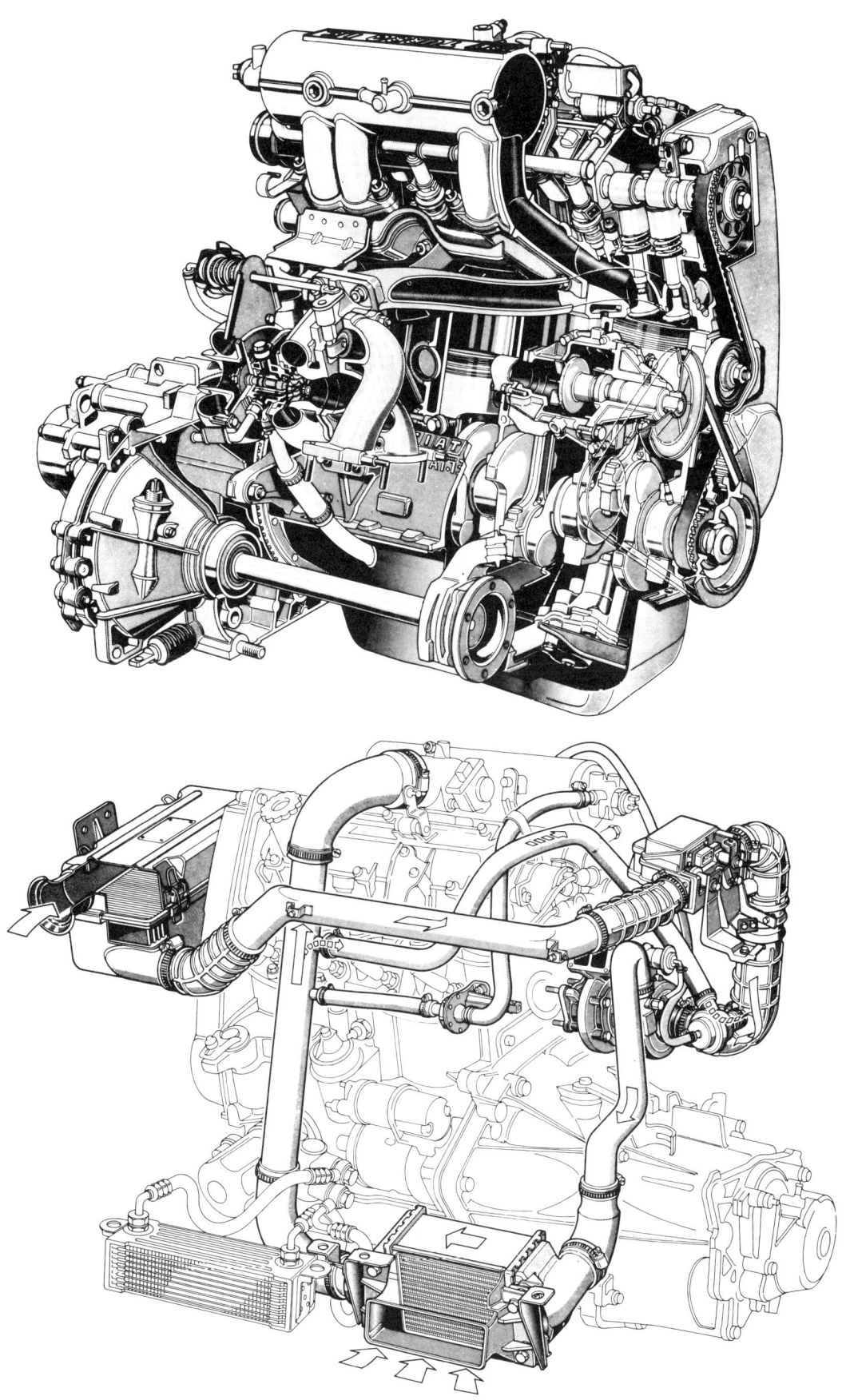

The 1299cc engine was specially designed to be turbocharged and was the only one of its class to offer electronic fuel injection, mapped electronic ignition with knock sensor and turbocharger and intercooler.

VARIATIONS ON A THEME

The Alfa Romeo Arna was the product of the collaboration between Nissan and Alfa Romeo. Models on sale prior to the 1.5Ti and sold with the Alfa Romeo badge were the 1.2 and 1.3 models whose main attributes were good value for money. The 1.5Ti was the first model aimed at the sportier driver.

Unfortunately the body used was the uninspiring Cherry from Nissan, but underneath were the Italian bits, such as the engine, gearbox, part of the front suspension, wheels, tyres and front disc brakes, all of which came from the beloved, but extinct, Alfasud 1.5Ti.

The Arna 1.5Ti was very reminiscent of its spiritual ancestor with the snapping engine, slightly sticky gearchange and general overall feel, until, that is, a corner was taken at speed. No matter that Alfasud suspension was partly employed and that the engineers from Alfa Romeo had breathed over it, it just did not handle as well, being far less taut.

The driving position was good with the pedals perfectly placed for heeling and toeing. The steering, via the familiar three-spoke Alfasud wheel, was very positive. The hatch release catch was located next to the driver's seat, just as it was in the Alfasud. Unfortunately the dashboard was grim, being unattractive and dated.

There was not particularly good news for the rear passengers either, for the rear leg-room was very cramped, worse than that of many a super-mini.

The car never could never live down the defunct Alfasud's past and it was no surprise when it, and the Arna name, were quietly dropped from the Alfa Romeo range in the autumn of 1986.

The Alfa Arna Ti was the result of an unhappy collaboration between Alfa Romeo and Nissan.

It was the Alfasud engine used in the Arna Ti, the 1490cc twin-choke carburettors pushing out 95bhp.

The rear hatch lifted easily for access to the 8.7 cubic feet load area. With the rear seat folded down, 35 cubic feet of load could be carried.

VARIATIONS ON A THEME

As part of the Peugeot-Talbot Sport Group A development programme a 10 horsepower kit was made available which consisted of a modified cylinder head, new camshaft and fuel calibration unit that raised to 7000rpm the fuel cut-off point. As a result, the 105bhp was raised to 115bhp at 6900rpm with a torque peak of 103lb/ft at 4800rpm. Standing start acceleration times revealed virtually identical performance up to 70mph, but then the better breathing of the tuned car took it clearly ahead, to the point where, at 100mph, it was 4 secs in front.

Taking advantage of its corporate links with Peugeot, Citroen installed the Visa, a model that had sold over one million units since its introduction in 1978 and which had been continually developed, with the 205GTi engine and transmission. Called the Visa GTi its new engine developed 105bhp at

6250rpm and torque peak of 99lb/ft at 4000rpm, identical to the 205GTi's.

Externally, the Visa GTi had the usual aerodynamic paraphernalia add-ons such as front air dam, roof-mounted spoiler etc. as well as low profile Michelin MXV tyres on light alloy wheels.

The Peugeot 205 GTi engine (above) was given a cylinder head modification that allowed it to develop 10bhp more to 115bhp. In the Citroen Visa GTi, the same engine, but without the cylinder head modification, was used, but the Visa GTi did not have quite the performance capabilities of the Peugeot.

The Citroen Visa GTi got low profile 185/60×13 Michelin MXVs on light alloy wheels, wheel arch extensions, all black window surrounds and roof-mounted spoiler.

The Visa GTi did away with the usual Citroen satellite switchgear and had the more conventional stalks on either side of the steering wheel. The instrumentation was clear and comprehensive.

The 1987 Citroen Visa GTi (overleaf) finally received the updated Peugeot engine which now developed 115bhp. Claimed top speed was now 119mph.

VARIATIONS ON A THEME

VARIATIONS ON A THEME

The car was not as fast as the Peugeot, its 0-60mph reached in 9.7 secs, 0-100mph taking 41.6 secs and a top speed of 112mph, but was comparable to the XR2 and MG Metro Turbo.

Economy was below average at 28.8mpg but over 30mpg was possible at touring speeds, but with a tank capacity of 9.4 gallons, it did not have the range of even 300 miles.

Its greatest assets were handling and ride comfort which were above the class average. Despite the low profile tyres and stiffer suspension, the engineers had somehow contrived to make it a comfortable car. With its five doors and respectable performance it was aimed more at the family man who needed more space than the Peugeot offered yet proudly claim that the Visa GTi, with the same engine, was little more than a five-door version of the Peugeot. Priced at a very competitive £5899 when introduced into Britain in July, 1985, it was considerably cheaper than the 2.0 MG Maestro (£7526) and the Alfa Romeo 33 Gold Cloverleaf (£6650).

Volkswagen were not standing still either having seen the opposition catch up, and in one or two cases even claim its title as best hot hatchback. Their answer was the 16-valve engine, announced in the summer of 1985 and introduced into Britain in September 1986.

As expected of Volkswagen, a spoilers and stripes route was not followed and it was a very understated car, as had been all GTis. It did not shout about its multi-valve head, the only difference between it and the more standard GTi being the alloy wheels, the deeper front spoiler and small red 16V badges on the front and rear of the car. It was enough, though, for drivers of the lesser GTi to ease back from the rear bumper once the insignia was spotted, a mark of respect generally accorded to no other car, whether in the same class or not.

The Volkswagen Golf 16-valve had a top speed of 130mph and 0–60mph acceleration in 7.5 secs.

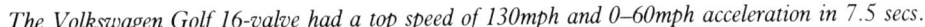

Producing 139bhp, the 16-valve engine was a development of the 1.8 fuel injected unit.

VARIATIONS ON A THEME

VARIATIONS ON A THEME

The 16 valve Golf was certainly a lot faster than it looked, and could reach a top speed of 130mph and a 0-60mph time of 7.5 secs. To recreate the cult car appeal of the first GTi, however, the marvellous 139bhp would not have been enough for the job so it was matched with a rather sophisticated trim package such as electric windows, a central locking system and a Blaupunkt stereo system. It meant, though, rather a hefty price rise over the standard model. The aim was not just to re-establish the Golf as the fastest hatchback but also to take on the class above and go for the Three Series BMWs and smaller Mercedes.

Volkswagen engineers had tried turbocharging the 1.6 litre unit as early as 1979 which they fitted to a batch of 50 Sciroccos. Developing 142bhp the unit was too thirsty and too inflexible at low revs and so was axed, perhaps a mite too soon seeing what Ford had done with their subsequent efforts at turbocharging, and attention turned to the 16-valve which had its official debut in a Scirocco GTX at the 1983 Frankfurt Show.

The fact that the 139bhp 1.8 litre GTi engine went into production over two years after its much acclaimed presentation in September 1983 was due to a number of technical difficulties encountered during the second half of the development process. With space at a premium below the bonnet, the second cam needed for the 16 valves was driven off the end of the other one which itself was driven by a toothed belt from the crankshaft. It took a costly and time-consuming measure to cure the troublesome belt with a short roller chain and helical spur gear.

With an increase of maximum torque of eight per cent, now producing 133lb/ft at 6100rpm, it was the power at the higher end of the rev range that was distinctively better, although it remained superbly flexible and could be driven around town without any problem. Ratios in the gearbox remained the same except for fifth gear which now became slightly lower resulting in it becoming less of an overdrive gear. The new Golf had a good economy achieving an average mpg figure of 28 which gave it a range of over 300 miles with its 12.1 gallon tank.

The Golf's virtues had always been its performance and handling. With the chassis being able to take extra power with the use of uprated springs, which meant that it was lower to the ground by just under half an inch, it was still a joy to drive. The steering at parking speeds was a little on the heavy side, but at speed, was well balanced. The ride was more stiff, but not unpleasantly so. It still understeered at highish cornering speeds, but became

neutral before the tyres lost their grip. The brakes were first class and used larger pistons fitted to the calipers. Extra holes cut into the front spoiler also helped in cooling the brakes.

Another important feature, seeing the opposition it was eyeing, was the high degree of refinement inside. The dashboard layout was excellent, and was second to none in this department and the pedals were ideal for heeling and toeing.

Overall driver comfort was increased with good seats that could be adjusted to obtain a good position for the steering wheel and pedal relationship. Visibility to the front was good, but the B and C pillars obscured much of the vision to the rear. The rear seat legroom was sufficient.

Introduced into Britain in September, 1986, the car was priced at £10,894. In performance its close rivals were the recently introduced Renault 5 GT Turbo (£7695) and the Ford Escort RS Turbo (£10,028), and such was the attributes of them all, that it would more than likely be price that was the deciding factor.

From all major European and Japanese manufacturers, there were now models competing in the hot hatchback market, which was becoming increasingly larger, not just with the greater numbers, but through different specifications, greater price differentials and emphasis on different aspects of a model's attributes. The German, French, Italian and Japanese could thus justifiably claim to have the best hot hatchback in the world, with not one competing directly against the other.

The 16-valve twin cam engine of the Golf was very potent.

The Golf GTi 16V was a very understated car.

CHAPTER SIX

THE NEW WAVE

While Austin Rover's big facelift of the MG Metro and Metro Turbo was confined to painting them all white, the French state-owned company, Renault, got on with the job of introducing new models.

The 5GT Turbo had already been introduced on the continent when it took its bow at the Belfast Motor Show in February, 1986. Its 1397cc unit was a bored-out version of the 1289cc engine and quite a bit lighter than any of its rivals with a light-alloy head on cast-iron block and wet cylinder liners. The valves continued to be operated via a chain-driven side-mounted camshaft through pushrods and rockers. The turbocharger was the small Garrett T2 unit, blowing through an air-to-air intercooler to a Solex carburettor. The engine ran with a 7.9:1 compression ratio and maximum 10.3psi turbo boost, which produced 115bhp at 5750rpm and a torque of 121lb/ft at 3000rpm.

With a top speed of 125mph, the Renault 5 GT Turbo set new standards of performance in the super-mini class.

The Renault 5 GT Turbo was due to get a 16-valve version of Renault's 1721cc engine in 1987, gaining 15bhp more to 130bhp.

With the power coming on tap earlier, 0-60mph times were attained in a startling 7.1 secs. Speeds through the gears were 37, 63, 87 and 119mph in fourth at the 7000rpm red line. These sporting gear ratios, combined with the excellent gearchange, allowed the engine's performance always to be fully exploited.

The 5GT's chassis had been extensively modified to cope with the extra power and an auxiliary 1.5-gallon tank coupled to the main fuel tank extended the car's range, but with an average 25mpg fuel consumption, it was still only a little over 200 miles.

On the road its stability was its main virtue, although cornering was good. Understeering was its main trait but it was less than a powerful engine in a smallish body might suggest. Momentary tail-slide could be achieved by taking your foot off the accelerator in mid-corner. Ride comfort was good, the stiff springs acceptable for this type of car.

The interior was a little like the curate's egg. On the plus side were the comfortable, Renault-designed, seats and excellent driving position, but on the negative side, the dashboard was a bit plasticky and the back was very cramped for passengers. Boot space, though, was reasonable and could be expanded with the split rear seat folding forward.

The Renault, like the Fiat Uno Turbo, was now on a par with the Peugeot in every way and only its relatively high price of £7360, against that of £6665 for the MG Metro Turbo and £7165 for the Fiat, was its major minus point.

THE NEW WAVE

Ford were another company who facelifted some of their range, the new look Escorts and Orions going on sale on 1st March, 1986. The nose was more sloped and the interior was improved throughout the range. The RS Turbo, from the fire-breathing racer in a smooth suit, was transformed into a more refined and civilised machine; so much so that it seemed as if Ford had dulled the performance edge of one of the

best hot hatchbacks around on purpose.

After the original RS Turbo, the new model felt slightly disappointing. Although impressive enough, it had lost some of the edge and urgency and with the increase in price, to £10,028, it now represented something of an expensive car compared to other hot hatchbacks and in particular from the Lancia Delta HF Turbo i.e. which offered more for over £1000 less.

THE NEW WAVE

It was in June 1986 that Honda re-introduced the Civic CRX, but replacing the 3-valve-per-cylinder 1500cc engine with a 16-valve, twin-cam 1590cc unit equipped with the PGM fuel injection which developed 125bhp at 6500rpm and a maximum torque of 103lb/ft at a screaming 5500rpm.

Experience gained from Formula One was used to good advantage in this engine. The unit itself came from the Prelude, but with the capacity increased from 1488cc and the weight reduced on the all-aluminium engine.

Its performance was one of the car's strongest points. Having a top speed of 125mph and a 0-60mph figure of 8.0 secs. the figures were almost comparable to those of the 16-valve Golf. With a 7000rpm limit at the red line, the speeds in gears were 37, 62, 89 and 115mph. Fifth gear was geared for performance.

Despite its tremendous performance, the economy did not suffer. An average consumption of 30mpg was possible and 33mpg attainable when cruising on the motorway. It was thus superior to its nearest equivalent, the Renault 5 Turbo. The fuel tank held 9 gallons which gave the car a range of almost 300 miles.

In increasing the power, the handling and roadholding were not compromised, indeed, they were superior to that of the old model. Grip was phenomenal with its 185/60 x 14in radials, and with its moderate understeering at high speeds, felt very reassuring. Straight line stability was also exceptional for such a small car.

The interior was still essentially designed to be a two-seater and in this respect had less to offer than any other hatchback, being more of a rival to the Toyota MR2 and Fiat X1/9. With its opening rear door, the car was obviously going to appeal to the customer who would be looking at the likes of the Peugeot and Renault, and was able to offer splendid performance, handling and economy at a price only £495 more dear than the Peugeot and £690 more than the Renault 5 Turbo.

THE NEW WAVE

The 16-valve Honda CRX had an even neater body shape than its predecessor. The side skirts were now colour-keyed as were the bumpers, and the 185/60R14 low profile tyres were fitted onto new style aluminium wheels.

Lancia had spent a great deal of money, time, energy and money in the pursuit of four-wheel drive. The development of the innovative and successful Delta S4 rally car provided the technical expertise which was only coming to fruition in 1986 in ordinary production cars.

Following the Prisma, the Delta was the next model to receive four-wheel drive while at the same time receiving a revitalisation.

The basic shape remained unchanged to retain the identity of the Delta, but it was updated and tidied up by restyling the bumpers, adding a deeper, more pronounced, front integral spoiler incorporating air intakes and room for auxiliary lamps, and restyling the roof line to provide for a more aerodynamic rear profile. The turbocharged models also got mini side-skirts incorporating 'turbo' badging.

Lancia had packed a great deal of technology into the Delta HF 4WD and produced one of the hottest of the hot hatchbacks.

Capable of 123mph and a 0-60mph time of 8.8sec, the new Citroen BX GTi was the latest in this revived marque's offering in the hot hatchback market. After the disappointment of not receiving the BX Sport in right-hand drive, Citroen remedied the situation for their British market with the GTi.

Using the same 1905cc engine from the former BX19GT (now renamed 19TRS) it had Bosch LE3-Jetronic fuel injection so that power increased from 105bhp at 5600rpm to 125bhp at 5500rpm while torque rose from 119lb ft at 3000rpm to 128lb ft at 4500rpm.

Underneath, much of the running gear remained as before, but with a gearbox using slightly different ratios than on the 19GT and slightly higher overall gearing. Not only did the GTi widen the BX range, but with the 19GT now becoming the 19TRS, Citroen was able to offer this model in an estate form.

The Visa GTi was the last model in the Peugeot-

The Citroen BX GTi was powered by the transverse overhead camshaft 1905cc engine that was used in the 19GT, but it was now fitted with Bosch LE-3 Jetronic injection.

The instrumentation became more conventional, the rotating drum speedometer being replaced by dials.

THE NEW WAVE

THE NEW WAVE

Citroen to get the more powerful version of the 1580cc engine, with 115bhp instead of 105bhp for which a top speed 119mph was possible. The rest of the car remained as before.

As has been mentioned, the Golf GTi was now being propelled by a 16-valve engine, so in answer to this, a high-performance 130mph version of the Opel Kadett was being developed by General Motors in West Germany as an answer to the challenge.

The new model, badged as the GSi, had a 2 litre version of the single overhead camshaft Family II engine, although it was known that Opel were developing a four-valve version. The Mk IV version of the Bosch ignition/injection system was used, with a free-flow sports exhaust system. It was thought that the new , 2 litre version of the Family II engine in this tune produced around 130bhp at 6000rpm/ The existing 1.8 litre engine in the GSi and Vauxhall Astra GTE developed 115bhp at 5800rpm and 94lb/ft at 4800rpm.

The Opel Kadett GSi in Group A rallying form had an engine that developed 170bhp and had a top speed of 137mph.

With the 1987 Astra GTE getting a 2.0 litre injected engine, Vauxhall brought out the SRi to fill a gap in the range that was created. A second generation of the 1.8 litre injected unit was put into both the 3 and 5-door models.

THE NEW WAVE

The aerodynamic shape of the GTE seemed to lend itself more than other cars to styling exercises. One such was the 'Samurai' design which won a graphic design competition.

General Motors themselves also had a try in creating interesting graphics on this model. Christened 'Quick Silver', they showed a car at the 1986 Motor Show which had metallic paint blending from White Silver in the front to black at the rear. Irmscher body panels replaced the front and rear bumpers, rear quarters and front wing.

Another developed hot hatchback with a limited production run was the Polo G-Lader which was not imported into the UK because of lack of space for the brake servo. A supercharged 115bhp car, only 500 examples were made for sales mainly in Germany, with some going to France and Italy.

The standard Polo Coupé S had a top speed of 95mph and 0–60mph acceleration in 13.8 secs. The spoiler above the back window helped stability.

THE NEW WAVE

While familiar models were being updated, there were manufacturers still entering the hot hatchback market all the time. In the autumn of 1986, another two contenders threw their hats into the ring.

One was the Suzuki GTi, hardly a name associated with performance cars, but from the word go, it was a little tearaway.

With lessons learnt from their motorcycle engines, Suzuki took just two and a half years to develop their 1300cc, overhead camshaft engine. The most surprising aspect about it was that it was a 16-valve unit, the first time that such a configuration was to be found in such a small engine.

Needless to say, carburettors were dispensed with and Swift's computer-controlled EPI fuel injection installed. It could rev to the red line at 6800rpm quite happily, although it did sound a little thrashy and noisy as it worked harder. The output was 100bhp at 6600rpm and the torque of 80lb/ft peaked at 5500rpm. Translated into performance and acceleration figures, this meant the car had a top speed of 112mph and 0–60mph was achieved in 8.3 secs.

It had a five-speed gearbox which had close ratios so that even fifth gear was not so much an overdrive gear, but more for continued acceleration. The gearchange itself, though, was just a little sticky. The speeds attained in gears were 30mph in first, 55mph in second, 74mph in third and 100mph in fourth. For a 1300cc unit being able to achieve the same performance figures as a 1600cc meant there was quite a high consumption of fuel, but an average of 30mpg was pretty comparable to the Ford Fiesta XR2 which itself was about the best of its class.

On the move the car handled well, and was certainly better than any previous Suzuki. This was mainly due to the replacement of the ancient leaf-spring set-up by a three-link torsion beam rear suspension which consisted of trailing arms, transverse Panhard rod and coil springs. The car rode on 165/65R13 tyres. Ride comfort was very acceptable.

Inside, the driver was faced with a well laid out dashboard and sat in a comfortable, colour-contoured, seat. Leg-room for the rear passengers was cramped and the low roof-line left little head-room. The boot space was also cramped.

Externally the Swift GTi received improved aerodynamics. The nose was more rounded and came down to the grille, which was now narrower and flanked by faired-in headlights. There was an air dam at the front which had fog lights set into it on either side. The front and rear screens were bonded and the side windows were semi-flush. These all helped to keep the Cd factor down to 0.35. Although a small car, and cramped for space inside, it was a pleasure driving it and although a late entry, was knocking on Peugeot's, Renault's and Fiat's collective doors.

The other late entrant also came from Japan, but they were challenging the more senior class.

Mazda come straight in offering the Mazda 323 having four valves per cylinder, four-wheel drive, turbocharging and an ABS braking system. They were the first manufacturer offering the 'techno-hatch' breed of car to the British public in the hot hatchback sector of the market that now accounted for 100,000 units per annum.

The banning of the Group B supercars, such as the Peugeot 205T16 and Lancia Delta S4, from

The Suzuki Swift GTi was not only great fun to drive, it had good looks.

The Suzuki's 16-valve twin cam 1300cc engine developed 100bhp at 6600rpm.

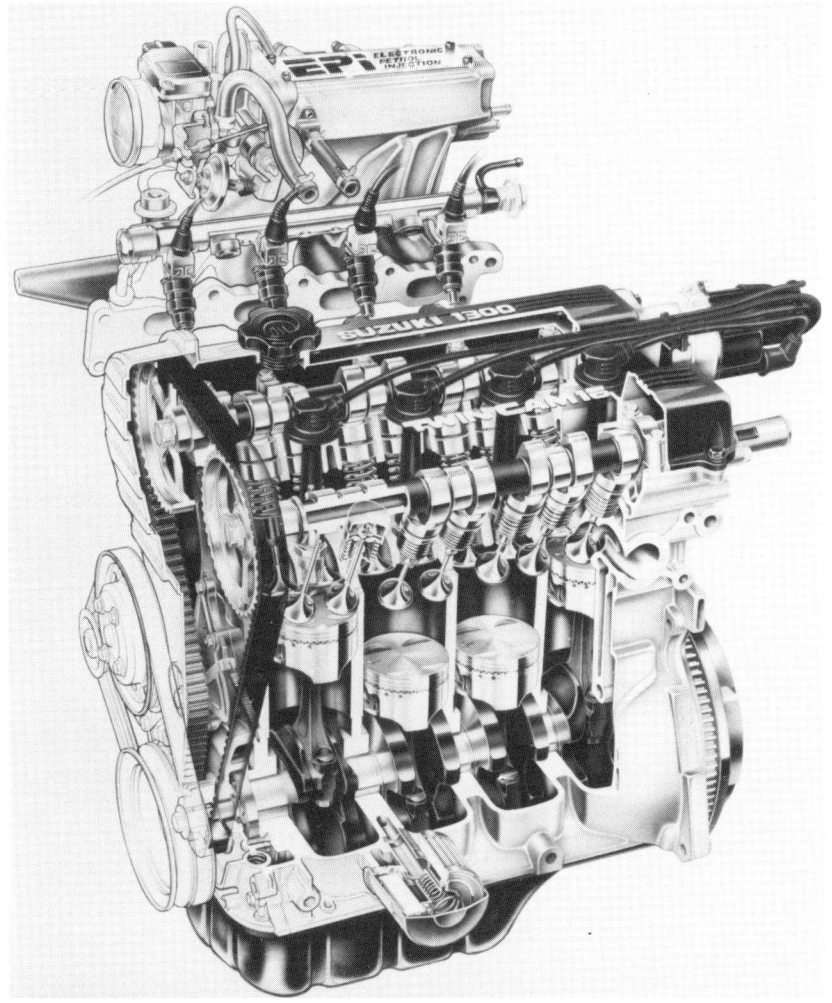

The Mazda 323 Turbo 4×4 (overleaf).

THE NEW WAVE

competing in international rallies from 1987, and switching the emphasis to Group A, where 5000 units had to be made annually to be eligible, caused Mazda to take a long hard look at their 323i model and see whether it could become the basis of a successful rally car.

The end result was hardly recognisable for the Mazda 323 Turbo 4×4 in one bound became a contender for outright honours in the hot hatchback market - but at a price.

There were two versions of the model, the Lux and Rally, the latter offering even less equipment than the Lux. Being the basis of a rally car, though, the handling and performance were excellent, but at the cost of ride comfort. The car was ideal for cross-country driving where the four-wheel drive, 50/50 torque split, system could come into its own, backed up ably by the ABS-type braking system.

The 1.6 litre unit, with the use of a water-cooled IHI RHB 5 turbocharger, air-to-air intercooler, electronic fuel injection and 4 valves per cylinder, developed 148bhp at 6000rpm and the torque of 144lb/ft at 5000rpm. Translated into performance figures, the car accelerated from standstill to 60mph in 7.9 secs, 0 to 100mph in 23.1 secs, and had a top speed of 120mph. Top speed in the first four gears were 33, 60, 89 and 113mph.

With the engine only too willing to rev up to the 6800rpm red line, fuel consumption could be a problem, and if an average of 22mpg could be achieved, it was quite a feat. When driven aggressively, consumption would fall to around 18mpg. With a fuel tank capacity of 11.6 gallons, it only had a range of 240 miles at best.

Even though a car of this nature was bought for its competition and sporting attributes, the low level of refinement and equipment were pretty pitiful for a car costing so much.

Its handling on the road more than made up for this and it was both safe and reassuring. On a dry road, it was almost impossible to get any oversteer, even when lifting off in mid-corner, and at the limit, would lift a rear wheel. On a rough track, the tail would hang out, but remained entirely controllable. This handling, coupled with the outstanding brakes, made the car well nigh unbeatable across country roads.

Priced at £11,750 the car at first sight seemed to offer good value for money with its sophisticated engine, four-wheel drive system and the braking system, but where it fell down miserably was in refinement and equipment, and although entertaining to drive on the rough stuff, it was not up to the challenge that the little Suzuki had thrown in the face of its peers.

The handling of the Mazda was impeccable along cross-country roads.

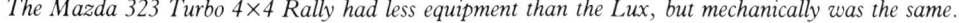

The 16-valve, twin cam, turbocharged unit in the Mazda produced 148bhp at 6000rpm and a torque of 143.8lb/ft at 5000rpm. Boost pressure was 8.1 psi.

The Mazda 323 Turbo 4×4 Rally had less equipment than the Lux, but mechanically was the same.

THE NEW WAVE

As with Volkswagen, Peugeot, still king of its class, was uprating its models in an effort to stop the whippersnappers pinching its crown.

In October, 1986 they announced that the 1.6 litre 205GTi would be joined in the New Year by a 1.9 litre-engined big brother. This meant that the power was increased to give 130bhp at 6000rpm and a torque peak of 119lb ft at 4750rpm. A top speed of 127mph and 0-60mph of 7.8sec was claimed by the manufacturers.

In the 10 years since the advent of the Golf GTi, the cult car from Germany had created an expanding and booming sector of the market that now looks permamently established. The danger is that as each manufacturer tries to outdo one another by having quicker, more technological advanced cars, the cars themselves will become increasingly more expensive and drift ever more into orbit and into other market segments. It was with this beginning to happen in the early '80s with the Golf size of car that allowed Peugeot with its 205GTi to come in underneath and partly steal VW's glory by creating a sub-division in the hot hatchback segment.

Now that VW are again uprating their Golf, Ford following with the RS Turbo, General Motors with the SRi, and with Peugeot trying to maintain its domination of its class by uprating its models, the whole market segment takes yet another half step up the ladder.

This could result in either one of two endings. Either it will be that the hot hatchback market will have climbed into a financial cul-de-sac where the

There was only one logo to differentiate the 1.9GTi from that of the 1.6, but the larger engined car also received different alloy wheels. Internally it got central locking and electric windows and mechanically was given a new set of gear ratios to cope with the extra power.

technologically laden cars will be too expensive for the enthusiastic, therefore generally younger, buyer to purchase them or else the vacuum left at the bottom, which was the original starting place of the Golf and 205 GTi's, will be filled by Japanese manufacturers who will then go on to mop up the rest of the segment altogether. It is by coming in at the bottom of the market, offering good value for their products, that the Japanese have traditionally taken over different markets.

The one sad thing, from the British point of view, is that where all major manufacturers from Europe and Japan are busy producing increasingly better models, Britain's state-owned car maker has a couple of uninspiring models in there which are begging to be developed further. And where we would expect to see more Japanese models coming along, almost every other month, we have nothing we can stand tall about from Austin Rover.

SPECIFICATIONS

Alfasud Hatchback 1.5

Max Speed		102mph
0–60mph		11.6 secs
Fuel Consumption:	Urban cycle	25.9mpg
	Steady 56mph	42.8mpg
	Steady 75mph	31.5mpg
Fuel tank capacity		11 galls
cc		Flat 4, 1490cc
bhp		84 at 5800rpm
torque		89lb/ft at 3500rpm
Fuel system		Carb
Length (ins)		156
Width (ins)		63
Height (ins)		54
Weight (cwt)		17.8
Boot cu. ft.		12/42

ALFA ROMEO ARNA 1.5 Ti

ALFA ROMEO 33 CLOVERLEAF

SPECIFICATIONS

	Alfa Romeo Arna 1.5Ti	Alfa Romeo 33 Green Cloverleaf
Max Speed	109mph	115mph
0–60mph	10.6 secs	9.7 secs
Fuel Consumption: Urban cycle	26.4mpg	25.9mpg
Steady 56mph	47.9mpg	45.6mpg
Steady 75mph	36.2mpg	35.8mpg
Fuel tank capacity	11 galls	11 galls
cc	Flat 4, 1490cc	Flat 4, 1490cc
bhp	95	105 at 6000rpm
torque	96	98 at 4000rpm
Fuel system	Carb	Carb
Length (ins)	159	158
Width (ins)	64	64
Height (ins)	58	53
Weight (cwt)	—	17.5
Boot cu. ft.	8/35	14/42

	Citroen Visa GT	Citroen Visa GTi
Max Speed	105mph	112mph
0–60mph	11.2 secs	9.7 secs
Fuel Consumption: Urban cycle		32.5mpg
Steady 56mph		47.9mpg
Steady 75mph		37.2mpg
Fuel tank capacity	8.8 galls	9.4 galls
cc	In line 4, 1360cc	In line 4, 1580cc
bhp	80 at 5800rpm	105 at 6250rpm
torque	79lb/ft at 2800rpm	99lb/ft at 4000rpm
Fuel system	Carb	Injection
Length (ins)	145	147
Width (ins)	60	60
Height (ins)	55	56
Weight (cwt)	16.5	17.1
Boot cu. ft.	10/24	10/24

SPECIFICATIONS

	Citroen BX GTi	**Daihatsu 1.0 Turbo**
Max Speed	123mph	100mph
0–60mph	8.8 secs	11.3 secs
Fuel Consumption: Urban cycle	27.2mpg	37.7mpg
Steady 56mph	46.3mpg	57.6mpg
Steady 75mph	34.4mpg	39.2mpg
Fuel tank capacity	14.5 galls	7.7 galls
cc	In line 4, 1905cc	In line 3, 993cc
bhp	125 at 5500rpm	68
torque	128 at 4500rpm	78
Fuel system	Injection	Turbo
Length (ins)	167	140
Width (ins)	66	61
Height (ins)	53	55
Weight (cwt)		13.9
Boot cu. ft.	16/51	5/30

		Fiat 127	Fiat Strada 105TC
Max Speed		95mph	103mph
0–60mph		13.8 secs	10.4 secs
Fuel Consumption:	Urban cycle		
	Steady 56mph		
	Steady 75mph		
Fuel tank capacity			
cc		In line 4, 1049cc	In line 4, 1585cc
bhp		70 at 6500rpm	105 at 6100rpm
torque		61lb/ft at 4500rpm	98lb/ft at 4000rpm
Fuel system		Carb	Carb
Length (ins)		143	158
Width (ins)		60	66
Height (ins)		53	54
Weight (cwt)		15.25	17.8
Boot cu. ft.		13/38	13/44

FIAT UNO TURBO 1.6

SPECIFICATIONS

	Fiat Strada Abarth 130TC	Fiat Uno Turbo
Max Speed	118mph	124mph
0–60mph	8.3 secs	8.3 secs
Fuel Consumption: Urban cycle	25.7mpg	31.7mpg
Steady 56mph	42.8mpg	48.7mpg
Steady 75mph	32.1mpg	37.2mpg
Fuel tank capacity	12.1 galls	10.9 galls
cc	In line 4, 1995cc	In line 4, 1299cc
bhp	130 at 5900rpm	105 at 5750rpm
torque	130lb/ft at 3600rpm	108lb/ft at 3200rpm
Fuel system	Carb	Turbo
Length (ins)	158	144
Width (ins)	65	61
Height (ins)	50	56
Weight (cwt)	18.7	16.6
Boot cu. ft.	13/44	9/35

	Ford Fiesta XR2 (old shape)	Ford Fiesta XR2 (Mark II)
Max Speed	104mph	110mph
0–60mph	9.4 secs	9.5 secs
Fuel Consumption: Urban cycle	28.2mpg	31.0mpg
Steady 56mph	43.5mpg	49.6mpg
Steady 75mph	32.8mpg	37.7mpg
Fuel tank capacity	7.5 galls	8.8 galls
cc	In line 4, 1597cc	In line 4, 1597cc
bhp	84 at 5500rpm	96 at 6000rpm
torque	91lb/ft at 2800rpm	97.4lb/ft at 4000rpm
Fuel system	Carb	Injection
Length (ins)	146	146
Width (ins)	62	68
Height (ins)	54	52
Weight (cwt)	16.5	16.5
Boot cu. ft.	7/42	7/32

FORD ESCORT XR3

SPECIFICATIONS

	Ford Escort XR3	Ford Escort XR3i
Max Speed	113mph	116mph
0–60mph	9.2 secs	8.6 secs
Fuel Consumption: Urban cycle	27.7mpg	28.8mpg
Steady 56mph	40.9mpg	45.6mpg
Steady 75mph	31.7mpg	35.8mpg
Fuel tank capacity	9.0 galls	10.5 galls
cc	In line 4, 1597cc	In line 4, 1597cc
bhp	96 at 6000rpm	105 at 6000rpm
torque	98lb/ft at 4000rpm	101lb/ft at 4800rpm
Fuel system	Carb	Injection
Length (ins)	159	159
Width (ins)	62	62
Height (ins)	52	52
Weight (cwt)	18.2	18.1
Boot cu. ft.	10/48	10/48

	Ford Escort RS1600i	Ford Escort Turbo RS
Max Speed	116mph	122mph
0–60mph	8.7 secs	7.9 secs
Fuel Consumption: Urban cycle	28.5mpg	25.0mpg
Steady 56mph	46.3mpg	35.3mpg
Steady 75mph	35.8mpg	30.7mpg
Fuel tank capacity	10.5 galls	10.6 galls
cc	In line 4, 1597cc	In line 4, 1597cc
bhp	115 at 6000rpm	130 at 6000rpm
torque	109lb/ft at 5250rpm	133lb/ft at 3000rpm
Fuel system	Injection	Turbo
Length (ins)	159	159
Width (ins)	62	65
Height (ins)	52	54
Weight (cwt)	18.1	
Boot cu. ft.	10/48	13/37

SPECIFICATIONS

	Honda Civic GT	Honda Civic CRX	Honda Civic CRX 1.6
Max Speed	112mph	117mph	125mph
0–60mph	8.9 secs	8.8 secs	8.0 secs
Fuel Consumption:			
Urban cycle	33.6mpg	34.0mpg	36.7mpg
Steady 56mph	47.9mpg	50.4mpg	52.3mpg
Steady 75mph	38.7mpg	41.5mpg	39.8mpg
Fuel tank capacity	9.9 galls	9.0 galls	9.0galls
cc	In line 4, 1488cc	In line 4, 1488cc	In line 4, 1590cc
bhp	99 at 5750rpm	100 at 5750rpm	125 at 6500rpm
torque	96lb/ft at 4500rpm	96lb/ft at 4500rpm	103lb/ft at 5500rpm
Fuel system	Injection	Injection	Injection
Length (ins)	150	144	148
Width (ins)	64	64	64
Height (ins)	53	51	51
Weight (cwt)	16.8	16.3	17.6
Boot cu. ft.	8/14	6.4	6.4

		Lancia Delta Turbo HF	Lancia Delta HF 4WD
Max Speed		122mph	127mph
0–60mph		9.5 secs	6.6 secs
Fuel Consumption:	Urban cycle	26.2mpg	
	Steady 56mph	41.5mpg	
	Steady 75mph	30.4mpg	
Fuel tank capacity		10.8 galls	12.5 galls
cc		In line 4, 1585cc	In line 4, 1995cc
bhp		130 at 5600rpm	165 at 5250rpm
torque		140lb/ft at 3700rpm	210lb/ft at 2750rpm
Fuel system		Turbo	Turbo
Length (ins)		153	153
Width (ins)		64	63
Height (ins)		54	54
Weight (cwt)		19.6	24.5
Boot cu. ft.		9/35	9/35

MAZDA 323 TURBO 4×4 LUX

SPECIFICATIONS

	Lancia Y10 Turbo	Mazda 323 Turbo 4×4
Max Speed	112mph	120mph
0–60mph	9.5 secs	7.9 secs
Fuel Consumption: Urban cycle	32.9mpg	25.4mpg
Steady 56mph	48.7mpg	37.1mpg
Steady 75mph	33.6mpg	28.8mpg
Fuel tank capacity	8.8 galls	11.6 galls
cc	In line 4, 1049cc	In line 4, 1597cc
bhp	85 at 5750rpm	148 at 6000rpm
torque	90lb/ft at 2750rpm	144lb/ft at 5000rpm
Fuel system	Turbo	Turbo
Length (ins)	134	157
Width (ins)	59	64
Height (ins)	56	54
Weight (cwt)	15.5	21.7
Boot cu. ft.		11/19

	MG Metro	**MG Metro Turbo**
Max Speed	100mph	110mph
0–60mph	12.2 secs	9.9 secs
Fuel Consumption: Urban cycle	35.1mpg	34.3mpg
Steady 56mph	55.5mpg	53.5mpg
Steady 75mph	41.9mpg	37.9mpg
Fuel tank capacity	7.8 galls	7.8 galls
cc	In line 4, 1275cc	In line 4, 1275cc
bhp	72 at 6000rpm	93
torque	73lb/ft at 4000rpm	85lb/ft
Fuel system	Carb	Turbo
Length (ins)	134	134
Width (ins)	61	61
Height (ins)	54	54
Weight (cwt)	15.9	16.6
Boot cu. ft.	8/34	8/34

MG METRO TURBO

SPECIFICATIONS

	MG Maestro 1600	MG Maestro 2.0 EFi
Max Speed	111mph	115mph
0–60mph	9.6 secs	8.7 secs
Fuel Consumption: Urban cycle		28.3mpg
Steady 56mph		47.4mpg
Steady 75mph		34.8mpg
Fuel tank capacity		11.0 galls
cc	In line 4, 1598cc	In line 4, 1994cc
bhp	103 at 6000rpm	115 at 5500rpm
torque	100lb/ft at 4000rpm	134lb/ft at 2800rpm
Fuel system	Carb	Injection
Length (ins)	159	160
Width (ins)	66	66
Height (ins)	56	56
Weight (cwt)	19.0	19.0
Boot cu. ft.	10/50	10/50

	Colt 1400 GLX Turbo	Colt 1600 Hatchback Turbo
Max Speed	105mph	121mph
0–60mph	9.9 secs	8.7 secs
Fuel Consumption: Urban cycle	36.6mpg	27.2mpg
Steady 56mph	43.1mpg	44.1mpg
Steady 75mph	32.1mpg	33.2mpg
Fuel tank capacity	8.8 galls	9.9 galls
cc	In line 4, 1410cc	In line 4, 1597cc
bhp	103 at 5000rpm	123 at 5500rpm
torque	114lb/ft at 3500rpm	137lb/ft at 3000rpm
Fuel system	Turbo	Turbo
Length (ins)	194	157
Width (ins)	62	64
Height (ins)	53	54
Weight (cwt)	16.78	18.3
Boot cu. ft.	6/34	

SPECIFICATIONS

	Nissan Cherry Turbo	Peugeot 205 GT
Max Speed	114mph	106mph
0–60mph	8.0 secs	11.3 secs
Fuel Consumption: Urban cycle		30.7mpg
Steady 56mph		54.3mpg
Steady 75mph		40.4mpg
Fuel tank capacity	11.0 galls	11.0 galls
cc	In line 4, 1488cc	In line 4, 1360cc
bhp	114 at 5600rpm	79
torque	120lb/ft at 3200rpm	81lb/ft
Fuel system	Turbo	Carb
Length (ins)	156	146
Width (ins)	63	62
Height (ins)	54	54
Weight (cwt)	17.4	15.9
Boot cu. ft.	7/15	8/42

	Peugeot 205 GTi	**Peugeot 205 GTi 1.9**
Max Speed	117mph	127mph
0–60mph	8.7 secs	7.8 secs
Fuel Consumption: Urban cycle	32.5mpg	30.7mpg
Steady 56mph	50.4mpg	47.9mpg
Steady 75mph	38.7mpg	37.7mpg
Fuel tank capacity	11.0	11.0 galls
cc	In line 4, 1580cc	In line 4, 1905cc
bhp	105 at 6250rpm	130 at 6000rpm
torque	99lb/ft at 4000rpm	118lb/ft at 4750rpm
Fuel system	Injection	Injection
Length (ins)	146	146
Width (ins)	62	62
Height (ins)	54	54
Weight (cwt)	16.7	16.7
Boot cu. ft.	8/42	8/42

PEUGEOT 205 1.9GTi

SPECIFICATIONS

	Renault 5 Gordini	Renault 5 Gordini Turbo
Max Speed	107mph	112mph
0–60mph	10.7 secs	9.8 secs
Fuel Consumption: Urban cycle	26.4mpg	31.0mpg
Steady 56mph	50.4mpg	44.8mpg
Steady 75mph	35.3mpg	33.2mpg
Fuel tank capacity	8.4 galls	8.4 galls
cc	In line 4, 1397cc	In line 4, 1397cc
bhp	93 at 6400rpm	110 at 6000rpm
torque	85.4lb/ft at 4000rpm	108lb/ft at 4000rpm
Fuel system	Carb	Turbo
Length (ins)	140	140
Width (ins)	60	60
Height (ins)	55	55
Weight (cwt)	16.2	16.7
Boot cu. ft.	12/27	12/27

	Renault 5 GT Turbo	Renault 11 Turbo
Max Speed	125mph	116mph
0–60mph	7.1 secs	8.8 secs
Fuel Consumption: Urban cycle	32.5mpg	31.7mpg
Steady 56mph	50.4mpg	45.6mpg
Steady 75mph	36.7mpg	35.8mpg
Fuel tank capacity	9.5 galls	10.3 galls
cc	In line 4, 1397cc	In line 4, 1397cc
bhp	115 at 5750rpm	105 at 5500rpm
torque	121lb/ft at 3000rpm	119lb/ft at 2500rpm
Fuel system	Turbo	Turbo
Length (ins)	141	156
Width (ins)	63	64
Height (ins)	54	55
Weight (cwt)	16.8	18.0
Boot cu. ft.	8/32	12/42

RENAULT 5 GORDINI TURBO

SPECIFICATIONS

	Suzuki Swift GTi	**Sunbeam 1600 ti**
Max Speed	112mph	107mph
0–60mph	8.3 secs	10.7 secs
Fuel Consumption: Urban cycle	38.7mpg	
Steady 56mph	50.4mpg	
Steady 75mph	39.8mpg	
Fuel tank capacity	7.3 galls	
cc	In line 4, 1298cc	In line 4, 1598cc
bhp	100 at 6600rpm	100 at 6000rpm
torque	80lb/ft at 5500rpm	96lb/ft at 4600rpm
Fuel system	Injection	Carb
Length (ins)	146	150
Width (ins)	61	63
Height (ins)	53	55
Weight (cwt)	14.8	17.87
Boot cu. ft.		14/42

	Sunbeam Lotus	Talbot Samba S
Max Speed	121mph	104mph
0–60mph	7.3 secs	11.7 secs
Fuel Consumption: Urban cycle	17.9mpg	30.4mpg
Steady 56mph	34.2mpg	47.9mpg
Steady 75mph	26.4mpg	37.7mpg
Fuel tank capacity	9.0 galls	8.8 galls
cc	In line 4, 2172cc	In line 4, 1360cc
bhp	150 at 5750rpm	79 at 5800rpm
torque	150lb/ft at 4500rpm	81lb/ft at 2800rpm
Fuel system	Carb	Carb
Length (ins)	150	138
Width (ins)	63	60
Height (ins)	55	53
Weight (cwt)	22.5	15.55
Boot cu. ft.	14/42	8/32

SPECIFICATIONS

	Toyota Corolla GT	**Vauxhall Chevette 2300HS**
Max Speed	118mph	115mph
0–60mph	7.7 secs	8.5 secs
Fuel Consumption: Urban cycle	32.1mpg	
Steady 56mph	47.1mpg	
Steady 75mph	34.4mpg	
Fuel tank capacity	11.0 galls	8.4 galls
cc	In line 4, 1587cc	In line 4, 2279cc
bhp	119 at 6600rpm	135 at 5500rpm
torque	103lb/ft at 5000rpm	134lb/ft at 4500rpm
Fuel system	Injection	Carb
Length (ins)	156	157
Width (ins)	65	62
Height (ins)	54	54
Weight (cwt)	18.9	19.9
Boot cu. ft.		12/34

	Vauxhall Astra GTE (old shape)	Vauxhall Astra GTE (Mk II)
Max Speed	116mph	121mph
0–60mph	9.2 secs	9.1 secs
Fuel Consumption: Urban cycle		25.2mpg
Steady 56mph		50.4mpg
Steady 75mph		39.2mpg
Fuel tank capacity	9.2 galls	11.4 galls
cc	In line 4, 1796cc	In line 4, 1796cc
bhp	115 at 5800rpm	115 at 5800rpm
torque	111lb/ft at 4800rpm	111lb/ft at 4800rpm
Fuel system	Injection	Injection
Length (ins)	157	157
Width (ins)	64	67
Height (ins)	53	55
Weight (cwt)	19.3	18.7
Boot cu. ft.	13/34	14/35

VAUXHALL ASTRA GTE

SPECIFICATIONS

	Vauxhall Nova SR	Volkswagen Polo Coupé S
Max Speed	96mph	95mph
0–60mph	11.7 secs	14.2 secs
Fuel Consumption: Urban cycle		36.7mpg
Steady 56mph		52.3mpg
Steady 75mph		39.3mpg
Fuel tank capacity	9.2 galls	9.2 galls
cc	In line 4, 1297cc	In line 4, 1272cc
bhp	70 at 5600rpm	55
torque	74.5lb/ft at 3800rpm	71lb/ft
Fuel system	Carb	Carb
Length (ins)	142	144
Width (ins)	60	63
Height (ins)	53	53
Weight (cwt)	15.7	14.3
Boot cu. ft.	7/29	10/37

	Volkswagen Golf 1.6	**Volkswagen Golf 1.8 (old shape)**
Max Speed	108mph	113mph
0–60mph	9.8 secs	8.3 secs
Fuel Consumption: Urban cycle		26.6mpg
Steady 56mph		47.9mpg
Steady 75mph		36.7mpg
Fuel tank capacity	9.9 galls	9.0 galls
cc	In line 4, 1588cc	In line 4, 1781cc
bhp	110 at 6100rpm	112 at 5800rpm
torque	96lb/ft at 5000rpm	109lb/ft at 3500rpm
Fuel system	Injection	Injection
Length (ins)	152	152
Width (ins)	64	64
Height (ins)	54	54
Weight (cwt)	15.94	17.2
Boot cu. ft.	12/24	12/24

SPECIFICATIONS

	Volkswagen Golf 1.8 (Mark II)	**Volkswagen Golf 16-valve**
Max Speed	114mph	130mph
0–60mph	8.6 secs	7.5 secs
Fuel Consumption: Urban cycle	27.4mpg	25.9mpg
Steady 56mph	48.7mpg	46.4mpg
Steady 75mph	37.2mpg	37.8mpg
Fuel tank capacity	12 galls	9 galls
cc	In line 4, 1781cc	In line 4, 1781cc
bhp	112 at 5500rpm	139
torque	114lb/ft at 3100rpm	133lb/ft at 6100rpm
Fuel system	Injection	Injection
Length (ins)	157	157
Width (ins)	66	66
Height (ins)	55	55
Weight (cwt)	19.7	18.9
Boot cu. ft.	14/50	14/50